AF322795

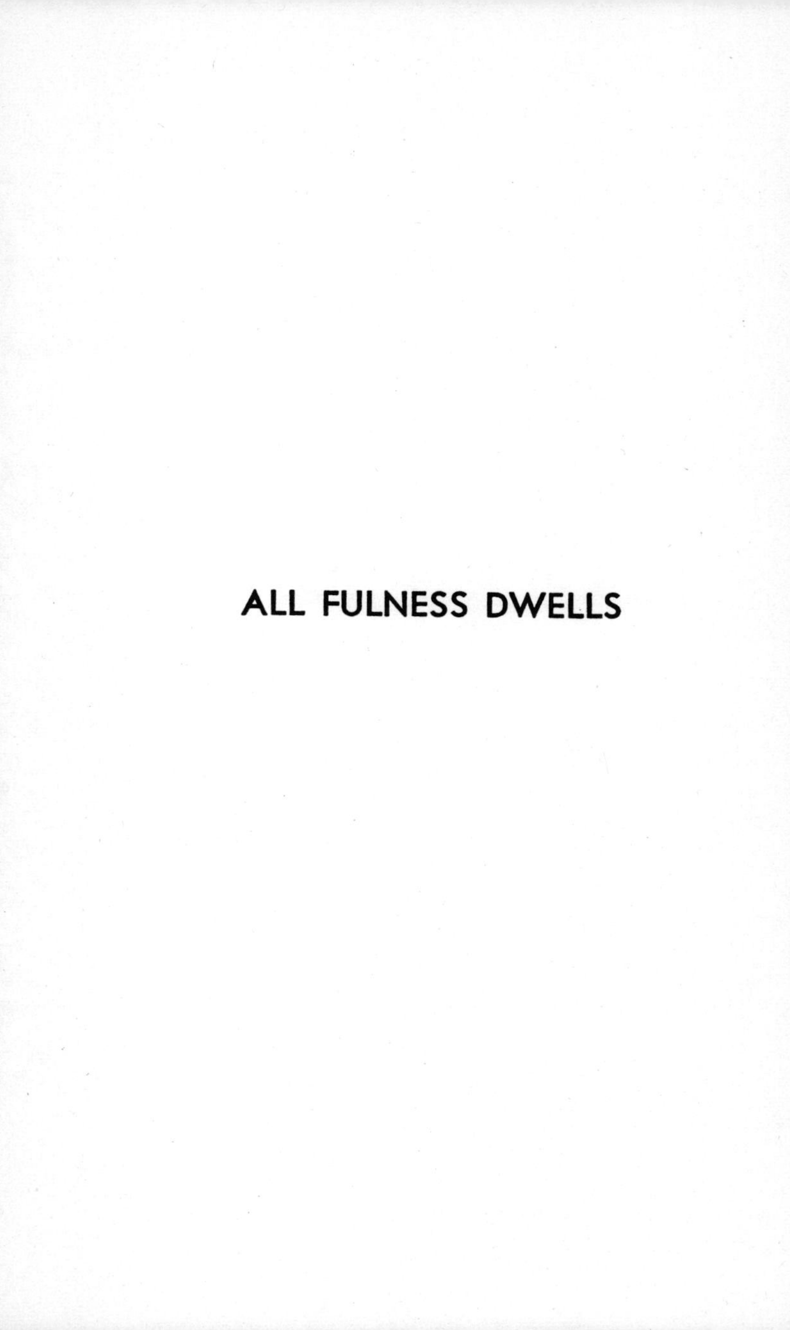

ALL FULNESS DWELLS

ALL FULNESS DWELLS

by

BOB JONES

BOB JONES UNIVERSITY PRESS
GREENVILLE, S. C. 29614

D E D I C A T E D

with love and admiration to

my father

who, without compromise, has preached

the Gospel

for over forty years

FOREWORD

I HAVE been reluctant to issue a book of sermons. However, because I have been so often asked if the messages herein contained —which have been preached many times in many parts of America—were available in print, I have consented to their publication in this volume under the title, *All Fulness Dwells*. Only one, "They Watched Him There," has previously been published elsewhere. This first appeared in the *Moody Monthly* and later in the *Winona Echoes* of 1941.

Some of the subjects have been so often discussed that it is almost impossible to throw any new light on them, as for instance, the Deity of Christ. But I have in all these messages tried to approach the subjects in my own way and to deal with them in my own style, and I have identified as to authorship the poems other than my own which are quoted herein.

I make no claim that these are deep, expository sermons, but I do claim that they are Scripturally founded. In each message I have sought to exalt the Lord Jesus Christ. He is presented as the Incarnate Son of God, as the Saviour of the world, as the Risen Lord, as the Compassionate One, as the All-Sufficient One, as the One to whom our service is due, as the One who prepares a heavenly home for us, as the King, coming to reign in power over His creation. I have endeavored to keep Jesus Christ the central figure of each message. My desire is that in turning these pages you will behold Him in whom "dwelleth all the fulness of the Godhead bodily."

B. J.

Bob Jones College
September 15, 1942

TABLE OF CONTENTS

1 1 1

GOD WITH US

Behold, a virgin shall be with child, and
shall bring forth a son, and they shall call
His name *Emmanuel*, which being inter-
preted is, *God with us.*

—Matthew 1: 23.

GOD WITH US

THE existence of God is a self-evident fact.
One has only to look about him at the wonders of the universe and at the beauties of
nature to realize that back of all the visible
creation is Deity who planned and wrought it.
The wonders of the heavenly bodies hanging
like myriad candles to light the capacious halls
of space reflect dimly the radiance of the divine
Mind which gives them light. The microscopic
life teeming in a drop of water evidences with
no less certainty the existence of the Author
of all life.

The Psalmist declares, "The fool hath said
in his heart, there is no God." In the face of
all the overwhelming evidence, the man who
denies the existence of the Creator is nothing
more than a fool. The Word of God, always so
accurate, says that it is in his *heart* that the
fool has said "there is no God." Despite all the
evidence which must convince the mind of the
fact of Deity, many men in their self-willed
hearts deny the existence of the eternal God.

The intellect cannot but recognize the presence and power of God in the universe. But
Deity, by the very fact of His existence, demands worship and obedience. Some men,
proud and rebellious, and unwilling to submit

themselves to these demands, *in their hearts*, where the pride and rebellion have their source, say there is no God. Such men, says the Bible, are "fools."

The *mind* of man cannot but recognize in the split-second accuracy of planetary motion, in the ordered sequence of the seasons, in the cycle of the processes of life in nature, the presence of a divine Mind, a divine Hand—a divine Lord. Truly, "the Heavens declare the glory of God and the firmament showeth His handiwork." The glory of God gleams in the pyrotechnics of the aurora borealis. The power of God is apparent when the storm rides the wings of the wind. The majesty of God is manifested when the earth which He created trembles in His presence and the earthquake shakes the rocks. The beauty of the rainbow, unfurled like a banner across the heavens, proclaims His residence in His universe.

But in all the manifestations of God through nature, God is a Being distant and far from human reach. The mind of man must recognize the existence of God, but the mind of man cannot discover Him. "Who by searching can find out God?" It is not necessary, however, that man discover Deity. God has revealed Himself in the person of His Son. The Lord Jesus Christ is God revealed for the appropriation of man's personal needs—his need of salvation from sin, his need of the limitless power of Deity imparted to him for daily living. Christ is the One who "hath broken down the middle wall of partition between us"—between God and man. He reconciles sinful man to a sinless God. He makes Omniscience available to lighten the darkness of human ignorance. He brings Omnipotence within the reach of mortal impotence.

The Lord Jesus Christ co-existent with the Father from the beginning, the One who John tells us was in the beginning with God, voluntarily took upon Himself the form of man that He might redeem man and reconcile him unto God. What great condescension to step from the realm of glory which had been eternally His into the tempest and turmoil of time! What condescension for God Himself, whose habitation is the universe, to robe Himself with the garment of flesh and the grave-clothes of humanity! Of His own will He came eagerly, gladly, unselfishly to die. Paul tells us that He, "for the joy that was set before Him endured the cross, despising the shame," and that it was for the death of the cross that He became incarnate.

> Countless stars bedeck the night,
>   Countless beauties clothe the earth;
> Thy hand set those lamps alight,
>   Thy Word gave all beauty birth.

Fairer than the stars of even
Shines the beauty of Thy face,
And no glories under heaven
Match the wonder of Thy grace.

When God in the person of the Lord Jesus Christ was incarnate among men, it was a complete identification of Deity with humanity—God in Christ became man, in all points like unto man except that He only of all the sons of man was completely free from sin. The Lord of glory became a child of earth. How great a mystery! The tiny Babe lying in the manger of Bethlehem was the One without whom was not anything made that was made. The tiny, chubby baby hand upon the cheek of the virgin mother was the hand of Him who holds the universe in the hollow of His hand. The baby arm about the mother's neck was the arm of the One whose everlasting arms are underneath all things. The lisping words of the toddling Child of Nazareth were the words of the One who spoke the earth into being and who created a universe by the Word of His mouth. The knowledge of the twelve-year-old Lad in the temple as He confounded and amazed the doctors of the law, was the knowledge of the One who is the Author of all truth and the embodiment of all wisdom. The One sitting on the well-curb to rest, tired with His journey and burning with the heat of the day, was the God who created the world in six days and rested on the seventh. The One who paid taxes to Cæsar was the One who established human government and from whose hand Cæsar received the power he so often misused.

In every point He entered into the feeling of our infirmities. More lonely and burdened than any other man was ever lonely and burdened, He prayed alone in the garden while His disciples slept. Thirsty, He asked for a drink of water beside the well of Samaria, and upon the cross He cried, "I thirst." Hungry, He resisted the temptation of Satan to turn stones into bread. Weary and worn, He slept in the stern of the boat amid the storm at sea.

Christ was incarnate for a definite purpose. He came to die. Man had sinned and man was under the condemnation of the righteous law of God. The human race had sinned and the sons of the race must be punished. No man could pay the penalty for the sins of man because no man was himself free from the condemnation of sin; but God Himself, the sinless One, in the person of His Son incarnate in the flesh, paid the penalty for the sins of man. "For this cause," said He, speaking of His death, "came I into the world." God did not become man to teach man how to live. Christ did not come into the world primarily to perform miracles—to restore the sight to the blind and hearing to the deaf, to send strength coursing through withered limbs. The miracles which He performed were indications of His Deity, the proofs of His power. They were the flowers which blossomed in His footprints as He journeyed toward the cross. In the Lord Jesus Christ the power and the love of God ally themselves in satisfying His law and in making divine mercy available for man through His atonement upon the cross for the sins of Adam's children.

> Thy habitation is eternity,
>   O high and holy One, who fillest space!
> Yet Thou didst deign to leave Thine own abode
>   And make with sinful man Thy dwelling-place.
> Thou, King of kings, didst put Thy glory by,
>   And lay aside Thy sceptre and Thy crown;
> Thou, everlasting Father, Prince of Peace,
>   To fleeting days and constant strife came down.
>
> And Thou didst walk with men and share their toil,
>   And feel their weariness and shed their tears;
> Thou, mighty Counsellor, didst speak Thy words
>   Of Heaven's wisdom unto foolish ears;
> And Thou wast patient with their ignorance,
>   Their stubbornness, their pride, their unbelief;
> Thou who art Life didst yield Thyself to death,
>   Thou, pure and sinless, hung beside a thief.*

The whole wonder of the Incarnation is this: it was for us, for you and for me, that God became flesh and dwelt among us. The personal application of His shed blood to our sinful hearts cleanses us; faith in Him imparts salvation to us. How wonderful that God

---

* Annie Johnson Flint.

should take upon Himself the form of man, become an inheritor of the "ills that flesh is heir to," suffer the ignominy of the cross; but how much more wonderful that He did this for us! The prophet Isaiah spoke for Israel when he said, "Unto us a Child is born, unto us a Son is given," but of a truth he spoke also for us, for all men of every kindred and tongue and tribe and nation in all the ages and of every clime. To shepherd and wise man, to the lowly and the mighty, to the ignorant and the learned, God reveals Himself in the person of His Son.

The stars were bright above the hillsides of Judea beyond where Bethlehem lay sleeping the drowsy sleep of its antiquity. Busy about their task of watching the flocks in the quiet of the cool, night air were a group of shepherds, humble men, born to a lowly task of earth—simple, humble herdsmen. The cold, distant stars looked down as on a myriad other nights. There were problems to be faced by the shepherds—problems common to all poor, lowly men of all times and all peoples—wives and children to be fed and clothed and cared for, taxes to be paid, a living to be made. All these were back of the nightly problem of the keeping of the sheep. There were wolves and other wild beasts that came up in the darkness. There were lambs that would wander away from the fold. There were injuries to hoof and hide. There was the problem of pasturage and good water. Little, petty, nagging problems! Faithfully they watched, stood to their task, these shepherds abiding in the field, keeping watch by night. To these men was the heaven a closed book save as it revealed the simple matters of direction—north, south, east, and west—or as it spoke to them of fair weather or rain on the morrow, or as the faint, rosy glow in the east betokened the coming of day. They could not read its mysteries, nor trace its planets in their courses, any more than they could explain the whims of the tyrant Cæsar or of some stupid sheep. Their needs were the needs common to men—the need of peace and love, the satisfaction of the hunger of the body, and the yearning of the soul. So, on this night, as on other countless nights, they watched, as their forefathers had watched in other years and other generations, the helpless flock. Alert, they glanced over the flock, wondering which ram would be taken by the Roman tax-gatherer and which young lamb was perfect enough for sacrifice.

Suddenly in the midst of the silence that wrapped them round like a cloak, there came a sound of heavenly doors rolled back, the light of an angelic face, the whiteness of seraphic robes. Startled, the men themselves, like their sheep at the coming of some wild beast, stood terror-stricken and afraid until the music of the heavenly visitor's voice poured over and around them in calm, soft melody: "Unto you is born this day in the city of David a Saviour, which is Christ the Lord. And this shall be a sign unto you; Ye shall find the babe wrapped in swaddling clothes, lying in a manger." And, then, from the suddenly-appearing choir, countless in number, came the antiphonal! "Glory to God in the highest, and on earth peace, goodwill toward men." The stars paled in the sky before the brightness of the angels. Like a wind across the desert sand was the noise of their pinions, and earthward came, fluttering like down, a benison from angels' wings.

Hurrying to Bethlehem the shepherds found all things as the angel had described them: the Babe, the manger, and the swaddling clothes; and when they had seen them, they made known abroad "the saying which was told them concerning the Child . . . and the shepherds returned, glorifying and praising God for all the things that they had heard and seen."

In the East were wise men—sages, scholars, scientists. From their towers nightly they studied the heavens. To them the stars were as an open book. The planets in their courses measured out to them the moments, nibbled from eternity by time. The comets were strange, heavenly visitors with whom they sought acquaintance, and who talked to them in a language shepherds could never understand. Faithfully these wise ones watched the heavens wherein were written in the burning fires of the stars the story of God's plan for man's redemption. But on one night the heavens with which they were so familiar burned with the light of a new star—"His star!" What a strange way to describe it, when all the stars are His stars, all the glistering suns chips and dust from the cuttings of the jewels for His diadem, swept out the high doorway of creation's workshop by a cherubic janitor with broom of fire; all the swiftly moving planets but whispered syllables from His mouth who spoke worlds into existence and "the entrance of whose Word giveth light." But in a strange, peculiar sense this was "His star"; for this star proclaimed His coming "from the brightness of heavenly glory to the darkness of earth's midnight pall." It spoke of the brightness of His rising upon the horizon of mortality—the Immortal One clothed with the garment of humanity—a Star of Hope for the sons of men in the night of despair. And, moving westward the star led them as they followed asking, "Where is He that is born King of the Jews? for we have seen His star in the

East, and are come to worship Him." To the shepherds the angel proclaimed a Saviour. To the wise men the star was the revelation of a King. How appropriate it was that to the keepers of the flocks, to those who raised the lambs for sacrifice, should be announced the coming of the Lamb of God, the Saviour of mankind; that to the wise men seeking wisdom and studying the wonders of creation He who is all wisdom and the Creator of all things should be revealed by an astral messenger, and that coming to worship the heavenly King they should be ushered into His presence by a starry chamberlain!

To those with ears untuned to the music of the spheres, He sent a heavenly choir. To the shepherds who could not read the secret mysteries of the diamond-starred script penned across the black velvet scroll of the sky, God sent an angelic messenger speaking in their own tongue. To the wise men He spoke in the language of their study and by means of a heavenly light. How appropriate the praise of the angels! How fitting the star! For He is the Light of light, "the true Light which lighteth every man that cometh into the world." He is the Giver of song: "He makes the woeful heart to sing," and puts a song of hope on the lips of sorrow and in the hearts of those bowed down with grief. So the shepherds came seeking a Saviour, and the wise men came seeking a King, and both found in Him the object of their search and the end of all their seeking. And the shepherds returned glorifying and praising God. The wise men in their wisdom went quietly away pondering in their hearts the wonder of God's mercy. The shepherds went out with a song of praise such as those only can sing who have seen the Saviour. The wise men left their gifts of gold and frankincense and myrrh at the feet of the infant King. The shepherds found Him wrapped in swaddling clothes, vestured in the cerements of the grave—this Infant born to die. The wise men brought spices for the burial of a King and incense for His funeral rites. Laid in a stable among the beasts of humility and sacrifice—the ox and the sheep and the dove—was God's little Lamb, the Heir of all creation, the Son of Man to die, the Lord of Life to reign! Humble toilers found the Saviour, and wise men worshiped the King.

> On the hillside, shepherds,
>   In the air, a song;
> And, amazed, the herdsmen
>   Behold an angel throng.
>
> In a far land, wise men,
>   In the night, a star
> Leading ever westward
>   Where Judah's bound'ries are.

> Shepherds in the manger
> Find the Lamb of God;
> A King waits the wise men
> At the end of their road.

So it is today, and so it has been through all the years since the Babe was laid in Bethlehem's manger. The needy find in Him the answer to the need. To all those who seeking find Him, He is the Saviour, and all truly wise men acknowledge Him as Lord of their lives. To the worker at his labor, to the scholar at his study—to the toiler at his task, to the student at his textbook—to the herdsman in the field, to the scientist in the laboratory, He is the only answer, the ultimate answer to human need.

Of all the names of Deity none sounds more melodious to the ear of needy men, none echoes more sweetly in the heart of God's children than this—"Immanuel, God with us!" In all the vicissitudes of mortal life, in the hour of sorrow as in the time of joy, amid war and poverty and pain and pestilence, as in peace and prosperity and happiness and health, He answers every need, giving strength and power, bringing comfort and courage, and affording wisdom and understanding. He is still, now and forever, "Immanuel, God with us."

WHOSE SON IS HE?

While the Pharisees were gathered together, Jesus asked them, saying, *What think ye of Christ? whose Son is He?*

—Matthew 22: 41, 42.

WHOSE SON IS HE?

"WHAT think ye of Christ? Whose Son is He?" These questions Jesus Christ put to the Pharisees. They, together with the Sadducees, had been questioning Him, trying to trap Him in His words. In the power of His divine wisdom He had avoided the pitfalls they dug, and He left them always amazed and marveling at His wisdom. Now, *He* questioned *them*, "What think ye of Christ? Whose Son is He?" They answered, "The Son of David." "He saith unto them, How then doth David in spirit call Him Lord, saying, The LORD said unto my Lord, Sit Thou on my right hand, till I make Thine enemies Thy footstool? If David then call Him Lord, how is He his son?" The Lord had done for the Pharisees in His two questions the same thing they had sought so often to do to Him, left them trapped in their answers, and from this time forth the cleverest of their lawyers dared no longer meet Him face to face with skillful questions. Matthew tells us, "No man was able to answer Him a word, neither durst any man from that day forth ask Him any more questions."

"What think ye of Christ?" Every one of us must face that question still. What do *you* think of Him? Certain facts of His life and ministry are set down in the Gospels. Reading those, studying the Gospels, you must come to one of four conclusions about the accuracy of the account of the life of Jesus of Nazareth and about His Personality and Deity.

First, you may dismiss entirely the historical accuracy of the record, deny the veracity of the account, and say that no such man ever existed, that He is the figment of the imagination of the writers, that Jesus as an historical character is entirely without foundation and fact. But, to take such a position is to deny unimpeachable historical evidence.

In the second place, you may accept the fact of Jesus. You may say, "Yes, I will admit He lived, that He was an unusual man, but I feel that the Gospel writers have idealized the portrait and exaggerated the unusual personality and powers of the man. I believe that here was a teacher whose disciples in order to gather followers for the cult which He established pictured Him in the record as a perfect individual, possessed of divine powers, neither of which He was." If you take this position you evidently are not familiar with the way in which the human mind works. Men are not accustomed to creating perfect gods. All the gods of pagan mythology, all the deities which man in all the periods of his history has created, have been shaped in the frailty of his own weakness. They have been victims of the same passions. Imperfect man has never made himself a perfect God.

In the third place, you may go still further and say, "I believe that Jesus of the Gospel record was a good man, a good teacher, perfect in wisdom and in kindness." In other words, you may believe the record is partially true. You may believe that Jesus Christ is a most unusual man, but not accept the Deity which He claimed and which is attributed to Him in the Gospels. This is the position held of many in our day—the unreasoning, illogical position of superficial thinkers. As has been often asked, if He were simply a good man and nothing more, why has the human race in its several thousand years of history never produced another like Him? In the positions of greatest eminence in every field of human achievement, no single figure stands alone. There have been great conquerors, but Alexander the Great must share his position of military and imperial glory with Cæsar the Triumphant and Napoleon the Victorious. On the pedestal of scientific greatness beside Galileo stand Newton and Pasteur. In the realm of music the names Haydn and Handel are spoken with equal reverence, and the three B's — Bach, Beethoven, and Brahms — alike compel our admiration. In the realm of great literature and poetry as loud as sounds the name of Shakespeare, to the fellowship of his literary immortality he must admit Goethe and Milton. In the realm of human achievement, human thought, and artistic endeavor, there is no one man who stands alone supreme; but as the one example of perfect humanity, as the only completely good man, Jesus Christ is without competitor. Surely, in the generations before and in the two thousand years since He appeared, had He been only a man and nothing more, there would have been some other son of humanity to challenge His position and demand by the accurate, perfect qualities of life and word the right to share His glory.

The fourth position in regard to Jesus Christ is the one to which reason and revelation and history impel us—the admission that He must have been the Son of God. On no other basis than this can we explain His perfection—He is "the only begotten Son of God." Everything about Him was unique. He appeared upon the stage of history at a time when Roman imperialism was at its zenith. He lived in a time when the philosophies of His day considered that might was right, and force was truth. He presented Himself to Israel as her King at a time when the Jewish nation was crying out for a sovereign of armed might and military powers to free from the sway of Rome.

He appeared at a time when hatred ran high and bitterness smouldered in the breasts of Jewry. Yet He made no effort to seize upon national sentiment to strengthen His position and gather a following. "Love your enemies," "Pray for them that despitefully use you," were the instructions which He gave to His followers. "My kingdom is not of this world." "They that take the sword shall perish with the sword." Yet, this was no idle, pacifist philosopher. Seeing the temple defiled by traffic and greed, He exclaimed, "My house shall be called the house of prayer; but ye have made it a den of thieves," and He drove out with the lash of a whip those who sold doves and overturned the table of the moneychangers.

He never sought popularity. He set Himself against the corruption of the scribes and the Pharisees and the priests. He became the champion of the cause of the poor. Yet he never fomented class strife nor neglected any need of any man—rich or poor, ignorant or scholarly, Jew or Samaritan. He dined with the rich and was called by His enemies a winebibber and a glutton, but He sought the outcast and the needy and ministered unto them. One of the signs which He pointed out to the disciples of John as an evidence that He was the Expected One was this: "The poor have the Gospel preached to them." He could not countenance hypocrisy and fraud. "Ye are like unto whited sepulchres, which indeed appear beautiful outward, but are within full of dead men's bones, and of all uncleanness," He said to the hypocritical religionist of His day. But to the poor creature taken in adultery, and by the law of Moses deserving of death, He spoke with tenderness, "Go, and sin no more."

His teaching was at variance with the popular philosophies of His day, as it has been at variance with the popular philosophies of every day. He taught that greatness was measured in service. "Whosoever will be chief among you, let him be your servant." Not the greatness of the gift, but the heart attitude of the giver He reckoned important. Two mites from the hand of a poor woman who gave all were greater than purses of gold from the coffers of those who, having given much, retained more. "Blessed are ye, when men shall revile you." This was His affirmation. "Whosoever shall smite thee on thy right cheek, turn to him the other also." "Forgive your enemies." These were His admonitions. Strange amid the selfishness and self-seeking of His day! Strange still to the practice of this world two thousand years since they were uttered!

Jesus Christ was born of the family and lineage of David, in the flesh a child of Abraham. His surroundings were Oriental and Jewish two millenniums removed from our twentieth century, but there is nothing typically Oriental or Jewish, nothing suggestive of a dead century about Him. In our day, as in His, the truths He taught prove their veracity where tested in practice. His lessons are just as applicable to our lives, and the solutions which He offered to the problems of His day answer the problems of ours. To the Anglo-Saxon He appears as an Anglo-Saxon. We never think of Him as having the qualities and characteristics of the Jew. To the Occidental He seems Occidental, and to the Oriental He appears a child of the East. Missionaries returning from the heart of Africa tell us that, when the darkness of the heathen heart has been illumined by His love, He is pictured in form and feature as a black man by the black man who has found his needs met in Him. The Chinese artist depicting the Saviour depicts a Chinaman.

His whole life evidenced His Deity. An angel chorus at His birth announced the arrival of the King of glory for His earthly sojourn. As a Lad of twelve He expounded Scriptures to the doctors of law in the temple, amazing them by His wisdom and His knowledge. At His baptism the riven skies, the descending dove, and the voice from heaven, saying, "This is My beloved Son, hear Him," marked Him as divine. He gathered about Him followers who moved in intimate contact with Him throughout His ministry — ordinary, common men. That they were convinced of His Deity there can be no doubt. That they accepted Him as God is beyond question. Many of them died for this faith. Peter, asked by the Master, "Whom say ye that I am?" sounded forth his faith with the words, "Thou art the Christ, the Son of the living God." Thomas beholding the risen Saviour cried, "My Lord and my God." And these ordinary men, transformed by contact with Him and fired by the truth of His Deity, went everywhere preaching the Word and thus changed the course of history. Universal in His appeal, hearts in every century and of every people respond to His love.

His miracles spoke eloquently of His Deity. He had power over the forces of Nature. The dining-room of a wedding feast became a laboratory as He turned water into wine. He had only to command the wind to cease and the waves to be still to calm a tempest and to quiet the sea, and cause the wondering disciples to inquire, "What manner of man is this, that even the winds and the sea obey Him!" The power of life and death was in His Word. He bade a fig-tree die and its withered leaves became a shroud for the dead branches. He called, "Lazarus, come forth," and the four-day tenant of the tomb responded to His command, and Lazarus went home with his sisters to help entertain their Divine Guest.

He had power over disease. Leprosy cleansed, sight restored, hearing renewed, lameness removed, pain eased, evidenced His healing power as the great Physician. The Powers of Darkness recognized and obeyed Him. Demons queried, "What have we to do with thee, Jesus, thou Son of God? art Thou come hither to torment us before the time?" And, when He commanded, "Go," they deserted the victim they had seized and he, by the Word of the Lord of Life, was released from the bondage of the Powers of Darkness.

With godlike simplicity Jesus Christ asserted His Deity. "I am the Light of the world." "I am the Bread which came down from Heaven." "I and My Father are one," said He. Beside the well of Samaria He revealed to the woman of Sychar that He was the looked-for Messiah, saying, "I that speak unto thee am He." He associated Himself with the God of eternity, when He used the name of the great I Am, saying of Himself, "Before Abraham was, I Am." As God He forgave sins and demonstrated His right to assume the divine prerogative of healing the body, saying, "For whether is easier, to say, Thy sins be forgiven thee; or to say, Arise, and walk?" From the cross in the hour of His anguish He spoke forgiveness to a dying thief and opened the door of Paradise for the poor malefactor suffering beside Him.

His Deity was so evidenced even in His death in the rending of the veil of the temple, the earthquake and darkness, that the centurion in charge of the crucifixion was compelled to exclaim, "Truly this was the Son of God."

What of His resurrection? So powerful was He that death could not hold Him; so divine that He could take up again the life which He had laid down willingly and return victorious over the power of death and the tomb. The grave clothes lying in their place, the stone rolled back, evidence but another time the Deity manifest in the life of Jesus Christ from the moment the Babe was laid in Bethlehem's manger.

His power in the lives of those who have acknowledged His Deity and been redeemed by His blood, is proof that He must indeed be the Son of God. A great host—they testify that He has done for them what only God's Son could do. A great cloud of witnesses—"a noble army: men and boys, the matron and the maid" in every century since He appeared upon our earth have trusted Him and proved Him God. By His divine power drunkards have been made sober, unclean men pure, thieves honest;

by His divine grace lives are transformed. He
is the Son of God!

>Thou whom seraphs joy in praising,
>   Thou whom heavenly hosts adore,
>Can my stammering tongue be silent
>   When I owe Thee so much more?
>
>Ever have they known Thy beauty,
>   Ever stood before Thy throne;
>But I wandered from Thy presence,
>   Separated and alone.
>
>All undone by sin and evil,
>   Child of condemnation, I.
>Yet Thou laid aside Thy glory
>   And for me came down to die.
>
>Heir of heaven Thou has made me,
>   Bought me with Thy precious blood;
>Took the form of man upon Thee
>   That I might be child of God.
>
>So, my song must swell the chorus
>   While the angels' praises ring;
>I, poor sinner, saved and pardoned,
>   Have more cause than they to sing.

WHAT SHALL WE HAVE?

Then answered Peter and said unto Him,
Behold, *we have forsaken all, and followed
Thee; what shall we have therefore?*

-Matthew 19: 27.

WHAT SHALL WE HAVE?

A RICH and apparently prominent young Jew came to Jesus with a question involving the most important matter with which any man is faced—the matter of eternal life. He came to the right One. He stood before the Lord of Life Himself, before Incarnate Deity, before the One who is the Giver of all life; but he recognized Him only as a teacher. "Good Master, what good thing shall I do, that I may have eternal life?" Jesus Christ ignored for the moment the question to challenge the salutation. "Why callest thou me good?" said He. "There is none good but One, that is God." Our Lord here implied, "You greet Me as a good teacher, nothing more. I cannot be a good teacher unless I am God." Over and over again the Lord had laid claim to Deity. If He were not God's Son, He was an imposter and a fraud. No such man could be a good teacher. Our Lord furthermore was impressing upon the mind of this upright but self-righteous young Israelite that only God is good, that the most upright and moral and honorable of men have no righteousness of their own to make them acceptable in the eye of a God who is all goodness.

Then he replied to the young man's question,

"Keep the commandments." From a young Israelite trained in the laws of Moses the next question may come as something of a surprise to us. "Which?" Surely he was familiar with the decalogue. Surely the moral law of the Old Testament was a familiar study. I think this young man, however, expected some new commandments from the lips of the Saviour. On another occasion when asked which is the greatest commandment He replied, "Thou shalt love the Lord thy God with all thy heart, and with all thy soul, and with all thy mind. This is the first and great commandment. And the second is like unto it, Thou shalt love thy neighbor as thyself." Feeling within himself a need and spiritual hunger unsatisfied as he sought to meet the obligations of the law, I think this young Israelite expected from the lips of Jesus some new law, some new practice, the exercise of which would bring him peace and assurance of salvation. If so, he was disappointed. The Lord answered his query, "Which?" by stating the six commandments of the decalogue dealing with man's relationships and obligation to his fellow man. "Thou shalt do no murder, Thou shalt not commit adultery, Thou shalt not steal, Thou shalt not bear false witness, Honor thy father and thy mother, and, Thou shalt love thy neighbor as thyself." The latter, I believe, a re-phrasing of the command against covetousness. He who loves his neighbor as himself will not covet anything that is his neighbor's, desiring that his neighbor have it as much as he desires it himself. Strange that the Scripture bears no record of our Lord's touching on the four commandments dealing with man's obligation to God. We must remember, however, that the Saviour was dealing with a self-righteous, moral, ethical young man.

"All these things have I kept from my youth up." Doubtless he thought he spoke the truth. There is no reason to attribute insincerity or dishonesty to the young man. Apparently his outward life had been in accord with God's law. Apparently he had maintained outwardly the right relationships to his fellow man. I am confident there was no stain of human blood upon his hands, no guilt of carnal sin upon his life. I believe his gold was honestly gotten; and, wealthy as he was, I doubt if he saw in another man's possessions something he desired for himself and which his money could not obtain for him.

But outward morality is not enough to meet the demands of God's righteousness. The standards of our Lord are always higher than overt action and outward practice. The man who hates his brother is a murderer in his heart, and to look on a woman to lust after her is to commit the sin of impurity, said Jesus; and He whose eye looks not on the outward appearance but on the heart of man saw the need in this soul for cleansing. No man by works of righteousness can justify himself in the sight of God. The disease of sin is inherent, and death by sin the inheritance of all the sons of Adam apart from divine grace manifest in the shed blood of Christ, the second Adam.

Seeing the need of the soul, Christ said to him, "If thou wilt be perfect, go and sell that thou hast, and give to the poor, and thou shalt have treasure in heaven: and come and follow Me." There was no salvation to be obtained in giving all that he possessed to the poor. The salvation was to be found in following Christ the Saviour. "Though I bestow all my goods to feed the poor, and though I give my body to be burned, and have not love," said Paul, "it profiteth me nothing." This young man could have converted all his possessions into gold, given the last coin to the needy, and then in penury starved to death, and still have been utterly lost. His salvation depended upon surrender to Christ. The numberless possessions to which he was enamored stood between him and acceptance of the Lordship of Christ. These must be surrendered if Christ was to be Lord.

The young man had come seeking to work out his salvation, asking "what good thing" he could do. By no good thing could salvation be obtained, but an act of surrender must be made. The young man was unwilling to make it and, heavy of heart, he went away. He turned his back on eternal life for temporal possessions. He denied the claims of Christ, preferring the lordship of Mammon. "He went away"—back to his palace in Jerusalem with its mosaic floor, with its walls covered with rich hangings. He went back to his fine wines and rich viands in silver goblet and on golden plate gleaming in the light of many lamps wherein burned fragrant oil. He went back to his silken garments and his soft couch. He went back to gold which he could handle and to the clank of silver in his hands.

He went back to the summer villa beyond the city wall, nestled amid the olive groves, with the marble porticos where soft breezes, perfumed by the flowers of his gardens and cooled by the waters of his fountains, caressed the garlands twined about the columns by his slaves. He went back to stand looking out over the fields of his waving grain like a golden sea rippling in the wind. He went back! He went back to be greeted by the trumpeting of his cattle and the bleating of his sheep. He went back to music and dancing, to the things which tempt the senses and mock the soul. He chose the things which in a few years he must give up anyway, when Death should pause before the portal of his palace or stop on the step of his country villa and call his name. He went back to those things which, if he lived long enough, he was to see destroyed by war when the Romans came; his palace leveled stone from stone, his villa burned with fire, his olive grove chopped down, his grain trampled under foot, his cattle slaughtered, his riches confiscated by the conqueror.

Poor, rich man! He lost immortal peace; his name is not set down in the Gospel record. He might have been a companion of the disciples, a messenger of the Gospel, but he chose riches. A robe of glory, treasure in heaven, might have been his; but he went back instead to things which moths destroy, and rust corrupts, and thieving fingers steal.

Riches in themselves are not a sin if rightly acquired. God sometimes entrusts His servants with great possessions. Money is not the root of evil. "The love of money is the root of all evil." Some men have gold more than they can count and do not grow to love it, but they are rare men. Some are enamored with the glitter and the clink of coin who have scarcely enough to rattle together in their pockets. The love of earthly possessions kept this young man from Christ. Gold became his god. In every life there is some overwhelming desire, some cherished plan, some selfish ambition, something which must be conquered, surrendered, and deserted if Christ is to be Lord. With this young man it was riches. With each of us it may be something else.

Watching the young man go away, the Saviour must have been sad at heart. God who never wastes an atom or an electron, God who had a purpose in all that He made, must be a God who is grieved by waste, and how sad the Saviour's heart must have been as He saw the wasted opportunities of this young man's life! Christ who came into the world to save sinners must have been grieved to see this rich and moral young sinner go away, lost and unsaved.

In that moment Peter chose to ask the question which is our text, "Behold, we have forsaken all, and followed Thee; what shall we have therefore?" What a question and what a time to ask it! Poor, blundering Peter, so gifted with the power of saying the wrong thing! Peter, who loved the Lord with all the devotion of his impetuous soul, but who could blunder so appallingly! He it was who, when the Lord spoke of His coming trial and death, said, "Be it far from Thee, Lord," trying to turn the Lord aside from the purpose for which

He had come into the world. But, Peter never said anything so inopportune, nor asked a question so base as this: "What shall we have for having done the thing you asked this rich man to do?" "What shall we have?" This was the question of the hireling and the servant, not the question of the disciple and friend; a question of greed and selfishness, not a question of devotion and love.

There were many ways in which Christ might have replied, and rebuked the question in the reply. He might have said, "Yes, Peter, you left all for Me, but have you ever thought what I gave up for you? I left the courts of glory and the palace of eternity, I left the adoration of angelic hosts, seraphic praise, and cherubic adulation. I left the presence of the Father and eternity My habitation, and sought the confines of this earth. I came to sojourn here among wicked men to be mocked and scorned, to be flogged and crucified. I came to suffer and to die. I laid aside glory for agony—for you. Yes, Peter, you forsook all, but what was that in comparison to what I gave up?" Had the Saviour spoken thus I do not doubt that Peter would have turned and gone away from the Master and the group of disciples and wept bitterly at the thought of his question, grieved that he had tried to discover the fulness of God's reward when he was reminded of the amazing love and grace of God toward him.

Or, the Saviour might have countered Peter's question with a question of His own. He might have said, "Have you forsaken all, Peter? Tell me, just what did you leave." I can imagine how Peter, taken aback for a moment by the directness of such a question, would have scratched his bushy, red head, and then burst out with, "Well, I left my house." He had. It was a fisherman's house on the beach. Surely, not a very prepossessing place, built of mud and driftwood possibly, and with sand for the floor and crude tile for the roof. And, how it must have smelled of fish! When he followed the Saviour, it must have been days before Peter got the smell of fish out of his garments and their scales out of his hair and beard. He left his house, a poor man's house, but home; and, after all, wealth and luxury are not requisite to home. The love of a mother kindles warmth and sets beauty aglow in a hovel, and a child's footprints in a sandy floor make a fisherman's hut precious and sacred.

He left his home. Journeying with the Saviour, when the curtains of evening were gathered across the sky, Peter saw the birds turn to the nests which they had built. As darkness gathered, the foxes sought the shelter of their holes, but Christ and Peter and the rest of that little band turned to the hillside, homeless. Peter left his fisherman's hut for the open spaces. Instead of the rough tile overhead was the distant canopy of night. No crude walls protected from the night wind. Instead of the sandy floor was the shale of the hillside. Instead of the bed of straw a grassy bank and a rock for a pillow. But, his bedfellow was the Son of God; and, I say, he made a good bargain when he left the house on the shore!

"Oh, yes, Lord, I left my nets, too." These were the tools of his trade. Rough nets of twine. If the catch was good the fish broke the nets, and after the night's fishing they must be mended. They cut his hands. They tangled easily. He left them on a rack on the beach in front of his house. It was good he did not try to take them along. How they would have weighted him down, how tripped him up, how tied him hand and foot had he sought to drag them with him, following Jesus. Peter was wiser than some of us are who try to hang on to the old life and hold fast to the things we should have left behind. He left his nets and the thrill of the catch.

But, one day on a hillside was a hungry throng. The hands of the Saviour took five loaves and two small fishes. He blessed and broke them, and from the humble lunch basket of a lad thousands were fed. Peter shared in that miracle. He watched those divine fingers break apart a tiny piece of fish and saw it become a lenten banquet for a multitude before his eyes, and Peter took the fish from the Saviour and fed the throng. That was more thrilling than to pull in a laden net aglitter with the fluttering silver denizens of the deep! Peter made a good bargain when he left his nets!

With sweet insistence the Saviour might have said, "And what else did you leave, Peter?" "Oh, yes, Lord, I left 'Nancy.'" It may not have been "Nancy." It may have been Rachel, or Rebecca, or Mary, or Elizabeth, but the fisherman's boat must have had a name. I can fancy how he left it beached on the sand, keel up. He had been called to be a fisher of men; and they are caught in busy market place, in town, and countryside. The waters of Galilee waited in vain for the boat.

But, one night, Peter and the rest were crossing the lake tempest-tossed in another boat sent by the Lord ahead of Him to the other side. In the midst of the storm Christ came walking on the water and Peter cried out, "Lord, if it be Thou, bid me come unto Thee on the water." Christ said, "Come," and Peter jumped from the boat. You ask how I know he jumped? I know Peter. There is no record of Peter's ever having done anything leisurely and with forethought. I cannot imagine the impetuous disciple putting one foot gingerly over the side and trying the surface of the water before trusting his weight upon it. Such a man would not have possessed the faith necessary to walking upon the water. Peter leaped from the boat. I can imagine how well he started his walk toward the Saviour, how he climbed to the crest of a great billow and skied down the other side. "But, when he saw the wind boisterous," his faith failed, and he sank. I fancy that he looked away from the Saviour toward the boat, that he wanted to be sure the other disciples were watching his progress. He could not resist the temptation of strutting a little. His faith became self-confidence, and looking toward the boat he saw the waves and he went down. "Lord, save me," he cried, and in that moment a hand reached out and Peter, grasping it, was pulled in from the gaping sea. The arm that upholds all the weight of worlds unnumbered went round him and he rested his hands on the shoulders of the Son of God and stood upheld on the surface of the raging sea and felt the calm of His divine presence amid the tumult of wind and waves. He left his fishing boat for moments such as this, and I say he made a good bargain!

But, the Lord did not answer Peter by reminding him of the glory which He had left.

He did not make Peter enumerate the things which he had forsaken and by counting them over see how unimportant they were. "He said unto *them*"—not Peter only, but the whole group. Peter had simply voiced the question which was in the mind of all. He answered *them* and through them answers *us* who question what we shall have who forsake all to follow Him. "And every one that hath forsaken houses, or brethren, or sisters, or father, or mother, or wife, or children, or lands, for My name's sake, shall receive an hundredfold, and shall inherit everlasting life. But many that are first shall be last; and the last shall be first." We have now the thrill of His companionship and the joy of His presence. We have all the abounding blessings He bestows upon His own. But, this is not all, though it were enough in itself. We have the promise of the reward to come.

Peter spoke truth. He had forsaken all. Most of us have left so little.

A fine young lady came into my office at Bob Jones College. She had just been to a music lesson, and she laid down her books and her violin on a chair. She said, "Dr. Bob, I need spiritual help. I came here to college to train myself for Christian service. I love the Lord, but I do not have the joy and satisfaction which I think I should feel."

"Have you surrendered your life to the Lord?" I asked her. "Have you given Him everything?"

"Oh, yes, everything!"

I walked over to the chair, opened the violin case, and took out the instrument. "How about this? Is this the Lord's?"

"I have given it to Him and told Him I will play it only for His glory."

"That is fine," I said. "It is God's violin for you to play for Him."

I put it back in the case, closed the lid, and snapped the clasp shut.

"But suppose He wants this. Suppose He wants the instrument shut away in its case. Suppose that instead of its song He wants silence. Suppose He wants the violin mute and not singing forth its melody."

She looked at me a moment. "I don't think God wants me to give up my music."

"I don't think so either. God gives us talents to use. The Book has something very definite to say about the sin of buried talent, but suppose in His own wisdom God wants you never to touch the violin again, are you willing to accept His will?"

She bit her lip and said, "No."

"Well, I think that is the source of your spiritual unrest, the reason for your lack of spiritual joy. You had better pray over that."

I saw her on the campus the next day, and the next. I do not think I ever saw a more unhappy face. The third day she was radiant. I did not say anything to her because I knew she would come back to the office. When she came in she said, "It is all settled. It is His violin. If He wants to burn it up, or break it into pieces, or cover it with dust, it is His."

That is an illustration of what it means to forsake all to follow Him. "Lord, we have forsaken all to follow Thee." Can you say that honestly? Leave the rest of the verse unuttered, the question unasked. "Lord, we have forsaken all to follow Thee. *Behold, how much we have therefore.*"

CHRIST AND THE CROWD

The Pharisees therefore said among themselves, Perceive ye how ye prevail nothing? *behold, the world is gone after him.*

—John 12: 19.

CHRIST AND THE CROWD

THE King of Glory entered the gates of Jerusalem riding upon the foal of an ass. Before Him the populace laid their garments in the way and with the waving of palm branches and with shouts of "Blessed is the King of Israel that cometh in the name of the Lord," they welcomed Him into the City of David. The Pharisees, jealous and fearful of His power over the people, beholding the scene, said among themselves, "Perceive ye how ye prevail nothing? behold, the world is gone after Him." The crowds followed Christ. Men of all circumstances were inevitably drawn to Him. He challenged the attention and waked the interest of all who crossed His path or heard of the wonders of His power. Over and over again we behold Him the center of the crowd. A woman who had suffered much at the hands of physicians and whose illness was still uncured touched Him for healing as He moved through the streets of a city with the throngs surging about Him, and the touch of faith brought health flowing into her through the hem of His garment. "Who touched me?" asked the Lord. "Peter and they that were with Him said, 'Master, the multitude throng Thee and press Thee, and sayest Thou, Who touched Me?' "

So great was the throng about Him as He entered Jericho one day that Zaccheus, short of stature, was unable to see Him for the press and ran before and climbed into a sycamore tree, that he might behold Him as He passed by.

By the shore of Galilee, they crowded upon Him. So thronged of the multitude was He that, in order to be heard of all, He went into a boat and was rowed out from the shore and, seated, gently rocking on the placid surface of Gennesaret beyond the pressure of the crowd, He taught the multitude.

Another day, on the high slopes of the hills that rose precipitously above the shores of the same inland sea, the crowd which had followed Him in great numbers all the day grew faint with hunger, and in tender compassion the thousands were miraculously fed by the Son of God.

He drew them by the force of His divine personality. He called the disciples and they came without question, forsaking all to follow Him. Little children toddled from the shelter of their mothers' garments and clambered from their arms to crowd about Him. Sinners looking into His face recognized a friend.

He drew by the wisdom of His words. The doctors of religion gathered in rapt attention about the Lad of twelve in the temple. Nicodemus brought his perplexities and spiritual problems to the light of the wisdom of the Son of Man.

Crowds thronged to Him, drawn by the miracles which He performed. They came— some to be healed, some to be fed, some hungry for the truth which fell from His lips, some driven by curiosity eager to behold the sensational and unusual. On the occasion of the triumphal entry into Jerusalem the reason for the enthusiasm of the populace is plainly set down. Those who had witnessed the raising of Lazarus had naturally spread abroad the story. "For this cause the people also met Him, for that they had heard that He had done this miracle." The problem was often how to get near Him. One poor bedridden man was lowered through the roof to find healing at His feet. They came with all manner of disease, halt and deaf and blind and, on one occasion, ten lepers came at once crying for healing to the Son of God.

Strange, sad sights the crowds must have presented; some on crutches, some unspeakably marred with festering sores, some barely able to drag themselves along, some borne by friends on litters, others sightless pushing their way toward the sound of His voice. They came; and there is no record that any having faith went away with his need unmet. The rich and the poor, the upright and the sinner, the publican and the nobleman, were all drawn toward Him. How the pressure of the crowd must have borne Him down! How weary He must have become from the pull upon His heart! The Gospel writer tells us that "He was moved with compassion on them." How the heart of the Saviour must have gone out to the meek and the poor! How He must have pitied the down-trodden and the oppressed, sheep without a shepherd, blind ones led of the blind! Constantly they pressed upon Him, until He, exhausted, slipped away from the crowd to rest and pray. Often He had to take the disciples apart into a quiet place to share with them the truths which were beyond the comprehension of the multitude and the understanding of the throng.

He walked the highways—up small streets and down,
  Or on the shore-roads by the glittering sea,
But whether in the country or the town
  They sought Him ceaselessly.
Men closed their shops—they left their plows to seek
  The many roads He took beneath the sun;
The women, eager to see Him—hear Him speak—
  Left every task undone,
Their little children stumbling at their side,
That all might see this Healer, Teacher, Guide.

That all might see Him! Oh, I wish today
  That He were here along some city street
Or country lane, and we could find the way
  On eager, stumbling feet:
Our men to leave their shops and plows to go—
  Our women every household task to find—
The One who had compassion long ago
  Upon the deaf and blind.
We are so deaf and blind—Dear God, I pray
That somewhere we shall find Him on the way.*

But, Christ who drew the crowd, lost the crowd. He spoke of a cross, of suffering, and death. He spoke of His body to be broken, bread for the soul; and His blood to be shed, wine of the new covenant. Some who had followed for loaves and fishes had no desire to drink of that cup or eat of that Bread. They came to take blessing and healing from His touch, but shrank from the curse of the cross. They came expecting to see the kingdom of Israel restored but were unwilling to go with Him the way of suffering which preceded the glory. On the day that they greeted Him with hosannas, with the sound of shouting and a carpet of cloaks, they cried, "Blessed is the *Kingdom* of our father David." The Kingdom and the blessing of the King they desired, and finding unpopularity and suffering lurking in the way which He must journey to His throne,

---

* Grace Noll Crowell.

they forsook Him to join with His enemies in the cry of "Crucify Him!"

It has ever been so. The multitude is eager to receive, eager to share in any blessing it can procure, surging around the man in the lime-light; but fleeing when the tide turns and unpopularity sweeps in, when cursing rises loud and hatred runs deep. Only the few are faithful in the time of opposition, amid the trying fires of rejection.

Down the years there have been many who professed themselves followers of Christ, when there was something to be gained by a connection with His Church and an association with His name, but whose profession was retracted and whose devotion failed when persecution raged and the enemies of Christ were in power. And, so it is today. Loving the world, Demas forsakes; greedy for gold, Judas denies; and fearful of His enemies, Peter follows afar off.

But the crowd will be regained. Because He "endured the cross, despising the shame," the Kingdom shall be His. Because He suffered, He shall reign. Because by His death He conquered, in the strong arm of His righteousness He shall sit enthroned, the multitude shall own Him Lord, kings shall lay their honors at His feet—the kingdoms of this world become the kingdoms of our Lord, and of His Christ. Because He bowed His back under the weight of the cross, every knee shall bow to Him. Because He as a sheep before the shearers was dumb and opened not His mouth, every tongue shall confess that Christ is Lord.

He draws them now—not the multitudes—but some hungry-hearted, needy ones, some who are willing to walk a narrow way and bear the shame of His cross. He draws them, some out of every "kingdom and tongue and nation"; but the day is coming when all the hosts of men shall acclaim Him, when the earth shall be full of the knowledge of God as waters that cover the sea, when all things shall be under His feet, His empire sweep from shore to shore, and when the words which His enemies, the Pharisees, spoke in bitterness that day amid the swelling hosannas shall have become truth—"Behold the world is gone after Him!"

THEY WATCHED HIM THERE

And when they were come unto a place called Golgotha . . . they crucified Him. . . . And sitting down *they watched Him there.*

—Matthew 27: 33, 35, 36.

THEY WATCHED HIM THERE

"AND sitting down they *watched* Him there." To some men it has been given to be a stander-by at one of the great events of history, an onlooker when the clock of time has struck some special hour. Men have stood by at the death-hour of great historical figures. His pupils and disciples were present when Socrates drank the hemlock. The Roman senators stood by dismayed or fled in terror when the conspirators stabbed Cæsar. Napoleon's death was witnessed but by a physician and some few attendants as he died in exile on St. Helena.

The crowd that gathered outside the walls of Jerusalem stood, however, at the midnight-hour of history — were witnesses of the greatest tragedy of all time and all eternity. They were present at an event marked red with a Saviour's blood in the calendar of the ages. It was a singular crowd that gathered there that day—Roman soldiers, the rabble of Jerusalem, strangers from the uttermost parts of the earth, proselytes, and those who had come out of curiosity to be at Jerusalem at the time of the celebration by the Jews of the passover feast, courtezans and priests, highwaymen and Pharisees, and those who loved the Saviour— all had come out to watch Him die.

The strangest thing about the whole tragic event was not so much that a good man should be executed between thieves, nor that the rabble should have come out to scoff at Him whom but a few days previously they had hailed as their King, the One come in the name of the Lord. Similar changes of popular favor have often occurred in the history of a fallen race, and the world's benefactors have often met such treatment at the hands of mankind unworthy of them. The strangest thing on this most sad occasion was the utter blindness, not so much of the crowd, but of the priests and Jewish scholars—those who knew the Old Testament Scriptures—and perhaps even of the Saviour's own disciples, to the meaning of the event that actually took place.

To the Roman soldiers gathered there in the strength of gleaming mail, this was the execution of a provincial agitator, the death of a fanatical teacher, and a stirrer-up of sedition; but in the eyes of God and the heavenly hosts this day was Golgotha a sacrificial altar, and the wooden beam lifted up the Lamb of God in the only all-sufficient sacrifice for human sin.

Watching Him there the rabble thought it was beholding the official execution of the decree of Pilate, the Roman governor, a sentence that day passed and that day executed. In their blindness none saw in this hour their prophecies fulfilled, but rabbi and Gentile alike failed to recognize that even before the world was, from before the foundation of the world, was He as a Lamb to be slain.

Smug in their garments of complacency and self-esteem, robed in their legalistic fringes, members of the priesthood looking on Him there saw in their bitterness and soured cynicism their vengeance wrecked upon One who had questioned their authority and upbraided their addition of vain ceremonies to the law of Moses and their accumulation of priestly vanities; but at the Place of the Skull that day was the High Priest Himself by sacrifice of Himself making full, perfect, and sufficient atonement. To this moment all the blood on Jewish altars shed had like a crimson carpet marked the way, and all the smoke of all the sacrificial fires since Abel's rough altar at the gate of Eden gathered in the cloud, which in His dying hour shut Him from sight of God and **men.**

To thoughtless ones within that crowd this was but the end of a man's life, a cruel end, but none the less an end; but in reality it was an end only to Satan's sway and death's dominion. It was not an end of life, but a beginning. To all who look that way in full surrender, and in faith for sin's forgiveness from Adam's time to this our day, and to the time when all things shall be put under His feet in His final triumph, this was the beginning of life *eternal*. Watching Him there they thought themselves beholders of the releasing of one spirit from the body of flesh, while in that moment was occurring the release of countless souls from death and hell.

To the lordly Roman standing in his pride in a vantage-point amid the crowd, this day but marked the removal of an influence inimical to the peace of Rome and her imperial sway. In human blindness and with eyes of flesh he could not see that in this hour was released a power that would shake the world, totter imperial Cæsar from his throne, and that the lowly Nazarene hanging in agony and dying on the cross would one day rule over an empire of which Cæsar's spreading domains would be but one small part.

In that crowd were doubtless some who had seen the Saviour's miracles of mercy, possibly some who had felt the touch and healing power of those hands now nailed upon the beam. Some there, without doubt, knew of His love and unfailing compassion, and watching Him die they may have said within themselves, "Love cannot prevail against hate!" Alas! poor, blind ones, they saw least of all, for in that hour was love most triumphant—God's love for man to thus give His Son—a Saviour's love to pour out His life-blood. In that hour of sacrificial love—love to His enemies who nailed Him there—was His heart broken and love poured out in water and in blood to wash away men's sins and redeem poor, erring sinners unto Himself, making them joint heirs with Him, the Elder Brother.

To some in the crowd who knew Him in His love and righteousness, looking at Him there may have come the conviction, "Today we are beholding the triumph of crime and oppression in the name of Law on this the Passover eve." They could not know that they were watching the Divine Mercy write an end of the Dispensation of the Law. They did not recognize the sacrifice of the Pascal Lamb, of which that lamb in Egypt was the type, or comprehend that His blood sprinkled on men's hearts would cause the wrath of God to pass them by as the angel of death passed over blood-sotted doorways in the land of Goshen. They did not comprehend that they were beholding God's justice triumph in the dawn of His redeeming grace.

To those depraved ones in the mob who howled to Him to prove His divinity by coming down, and to the thief beside Him railing, "If Thou be Christ save Thyself and us," His death was evidence of mortal weakness and mere humanity. They could not see that it was the power of His divine Omnipotence which made Him endure the Cross, despising the shame, nor could they know that His own divinity and not the nails in outstretched hands and pierced feet it was that held Him there. His followers had not understood His meaning when He said that no man took His life from Him, that He laid it down willingly.

When they heard Him cry, "Eli, eli, lama sabachthani?" some of that number thought it the agonizing cry of a dying man to a long-dead prophet. That cry, "My God, My God, why hast Thou forsaken Me?" was the saddest that ever rang in the ears of God or man—the cry of God Himself, the uncreated Son, a Person of the Trinity, One with the Father from the beginning as He for the first time in all eternity knew separation from the Father, covered in His agonies by the sins of all mankind He bore.

"*They* watched Him there."

In the hour of Christ's crucifixion human depravity was most manifest. Human depravity that made Calvary necessary most delighted in the death of Him who hung there for men's sins.

I do not like pictures of the crucifixion. It has never seemed to me that any artist could depict the scene with all its horrible detail and that no pitiful or unhardened man could look thereon without becoming ill. I have no use for those paintings, nor for the crucifix that pictures the pale ivory body of a fair-faced man against the dark background of the beam. I have stood in world-famous art galleries before canvases on which the greatest artists have attempted to depict the scene; I have seen how Rubens has treated the subject of the crucifixion and marveled at the lifelike qualities of the flesh tints that he used. Each of the great Italian Renaissance painters who dared attempt to catch with oils on canvas Golgotha's tragedy impresses me for some particular skill or technique in his art. The Dutch and German painters in the North, the British artists, and the great artists of our own country have each brought something of artistic worth and beauty of color as they have touched the crucifixion scene, but somehow they all leave me unsatisfied and fail to catch the horror and agony of the scene.

Each man can best see Him there as the Holy Spirit limns the picture in his soul. Isaiah prophetically looking forward beheld the Cross atop the brow of Golgotha and wrote, "And when we shall see Him, there is no beauty that we should desire Him." "His visage was so marred more than any man." Picture Him there one mass of blood, the flesh of His back torn through to the bone by the lash of Roman soldiers, His eyes almost closed in His face from the blows of the soldiers' fists, the blood from the thorn-crowned brow running down the beard, the torn hands, the pierced feet—the modest son of God held high aloft before the gaze of all that mob, clothed only with the garments of His blood and with the flies that settled like a crawling cloak across His quivering form. They watched Him there. They watched Him while He bore their sins, watched Him unmoved or mocking. They watched though God turned away His face. They watched until the Father drew a veil of darkness around His suffering form.

"They watched *Him* there."

I never read the account of the crucifixion as recorded in the Gospel but I marvel how that mob could stand unmoved in the presence of His death. Yet the only conversion recorded in the hour of His crucifixion was the conversion of the thief who hung beside Him against the sky, a conversion that sprang definitely, as every conversion must, from a sense of guilt. "Dost not thou fear God, seeing thou art in the same condemnation? and we indeed justly; for we receive the due reward of our deeds: but this man hath done nothing amiss." And, every one of us would have hung there that day had we with that poor thief received the due reward of our misdeeds. In his declamation that thief recognizing Christ's divinity and freedom from sin, the factors which made Him a satisfactory sacrifice, and recognizing and confessing his own sin felt the cleansing blood that has sufficed for all who have sought to wash their souls clean in its flow. Indeed, *we* should have suffered there. Not that Jewish mob that day, not those Roman soldiers, nor Pilate's order, nor the hostile Jewish priesthood, but *our* sins nailed Him there. With cruel hands *we* made the crown that pierced His brow out of the thorns of our wickedness and sin plucked from the stony ground of our own evil, godless hearts, and by our own rejection and denial of His kingly sway within our lives *we* wove the mocking thorns into His coronet. Each one of us has had a share in the blows that lashed His back; each blasphemy of an unregenerate tongue cut deeply into His flesh. He was stung by the thongs of our rebellion, cut deeply by the stubbornness of our pride and self-will, and as we look upon those hands and feet impaled there we might well cover our faces and cry out in shame to think *we* nailed Him there. Those hands that were never stretched out save in mercy, those hands that touched with healing and with love, those hands that made blind eyes to see and deaf ears to hear, those hands that in compassion touched the leper whom none else dared touch and led him back from living death to union with the ones he loved, those hands that knocked upon the tomb's portal as upon the doorway of a bedroom to wake the sleeper and send the dead back to sit beside the fires of home, those hands—*we* nailed them there. Those feet that walked so many weary miles on errands of mercy and grace, those holy feet that walked upon the water as the Saviour in the beginning had walked the pathways of the heavens amid the anthems of the singing morning stars, those feet — *we* nailed them there! Those nails were mined out of the evil pits and dark galleries of our vain, sinful thoughts, heated at the fires of our lusts, forged on the anvil of our hatred, and driven into His quivering flesh by the hammer of our depravity; each stinging, nerve-racking blow a sin that *we* committed.

That cross itself *we* made. A tree God planted to be a blessing, a shade and shelter, formed the beam on which He hung. A tree which might have been the rafter of a home to shelter a family from the storm, a tree which might have become the tall mast of a stout ship sailing in pride across the seas in service to mankind—that tree became a cross, but it was a cross *we* fashioned. Fashioned from the gifts God gave us perverted to our own selfish pleasure; from talents which, yielded to God, might have blessed the world but which we used for self and sinful gratification—fashioned from these was His cross.

Yes, with the thief we might have suffered, justly, for all the agony of those hours and all the anguish that He bore—not only the physical suffering of the body but also the suffering of the separation from the Father—were rightly ours, and in the anguish of the cross He endured all the anguish of hell of all lost men. Yes, they were likewise *ours—yours—mine*. We might have hung, had we received our own deserts, upon that cross, but in His mercy and His love, sitting down they watched Him there.

"They watched Him *there*."

It is no wonder that man in his sin and in his depravity hates the cross. It is not strange that Satan seeks to hide it with darkness blacker than that which covered it in the ninth hour when Christ having cried with a loud voice, "It is finished," yielded up the ghost; for only as we see Christ on the *cross* can we be saved, only as we watch Him *there* are we redeemed, only as we plunge in the blood there shed can sins be washed away. We watch Him in His ministry, a ministry like which there is no other—a ministry of healing and blessing. We watch Him in His miracles and marvel at His power and His love. We watch Him in His teaching, and we stand amazed in the presence of His wisdom and His brilliant simplicity of speech as He speaks as one having authority; but it is only as sinful man watches Him *there* that he knows Him in the purpose for which He came into this world, and that it is only as sinful man watches Him *there* that he can claim Him as his Saviour. The last time the sinful world ever saw Him, He hung there. Only the redeemed beheld Him in the glory of His resurrection.

His shed blood is the *leitmotif* of Scripture, the theme of heavenly song, the boast of the redeemed. Calvary is the focal point of human history, the holy mount of God's heavenly kingdom, where man may enter into Divine presence, the natal chamber where children are born into the family of God. It is at Golgotha that law, whereby man seeks to climb to fellowship with the Father, meets grace, which lifts him there. Calvary is the axis of eternity, the jewel of earth's diadem. To the Christian in the presence of the Cross all the problems of life are settled. Here all temptations are withstood and Satan met here is here defeated and only here does overcoming strength abound. The Christian cannot look long upon the Cross or watch Him there without becoming conscious that the world that crucified the Saviour has nothing of value to offer him. Temporal things viewed in the light that streams from Calvary will seem as garish and as tawdry as they are. To the sinner Calvary is the only hope, the Saviour on the Cross the only plea for pardon which can reach the ears of God. Behold Him there!

> When I survey the wondrous Cross
>   On which the Prince of glory died,
> My richest gain I count but loss,
>   And pour contempt on all my pride.
>
> Forbid it, Lord, that I should boast
>   Save in the death of Christ, my God;
> All the vain things that charm me most,
>   I sacrifice them to His blood.
>
> See, from His head, His hands, His feet,
>   Sorrow and love flow mingled down;
> Did e'er such love and sorrow meet,
>   Or thorns compose so rich a crown?
>
> His dying crimson, like a robe,
>   Spreads o'er His body on the tree;
> Then I am dead to all the globe,
>   And all the globe is dead to me.
>
> Were the whole realm of nature mine,
>   That were a present far too small;
> Love so amazing, so divine,
>   Demands my soul, my life, my all.*

---

* Isaac Watts.

A GARDEN IN THE PLACE

Now *in the place where He was crucified there was a garden;* and in the garden a new sepulchre, wherein was never man yet laid.

—John 19: 41.

A GARDEN IN THE PLACE

THE four Gospels in a few well-cut, crystal phrases, sparkling with the prismatic colors of radiant truth, give us the resurrection story. The four accounts taken together offer few details of the glorious event of that springtime morning. So wonderful, so marvelous is the fact of the resurrection of the Lord Jesus Christ that no metaphorical embellishment or ornamentation of words and phrases is needed to arrest the attention of the mind or capture the heart.

"Now is Christ risen from the dead . . . the first fruits of them that slept," thus Paul states the fact. The Word of God needs no proof. No arguments are necessary to prove the resurrection of our Lord. There is no better established fact of history than the fact of His resurrection. There is no better proof that Christ is risen from the dead than the resurrection power of the Lord Jesus Christ as it is manifest in the life of the believer.

The simple facts are these. The body of the Lord Jesus was laid in the tomb of Joseph of Arimathea, fulfilling the words of the prophet Isaiah, who said that He should be "with the rich in His death." That a crucified man should be given decent burial was in itself remarkable. We are told that Joseph went to Pilate and *begged* the body of Christ. The bodies of those dead by crucifixion, the Romans customarily left upon their crosses, food for the birds of the air, or they were taken down to be cast into a common pit, or thrown out into the open fields to be devoured by beasts of prey.

On the afternoon of the crucifixion, with the Sabbath drawing nigh, there was not time to prepare the body properly for burial. Temporary preparations were made therefore. Anointed with spices and hastily wrapped, the mortal tenement of the Son of God was sealed away and placed under Roman guard.

On the morning of the third day, the Sabbath being past, Mary Magdalene, Joanna, Mary the mother of James, and others came early in the morning to complete the anointing and embalming of the body for what they thought would be its long sleep in the tomb. Early they came, leaving their homes even before day, before the streets were crowded, or the busy city awake. They came as the morning began to dawn to complete the last loving task in their power to perform for the One whom they had loved. As they journeyed through the winding, narrow streets of Jerusalem and out beyond the gates toward the mount of execution and its garden near by, they wondered among themselves who would remove the stone from the sepulchre. The strength of a few weak women was insufficient for that task, but upon arriving they found that the removal of the stone was as unnecessary as the anointing of the body—that the one task had been accomplished and the other was now and forever unnecessary. They journeyed toward a guarded grave, but they found a tenantless tomb. They came expecting to find a sealed sepulchre, but there awaited them a burial-place barren of the body of their Beloved. They came in sorrow and were seized with fear when they beheld the angels and heard from those heavenly messengers the truth of the resurrection, evidenced in the abandoned cerements and deserted tomb, for they were not yet able to comprehend the truth of His resurrection.

The frightened and bewildered women came to Peter and John with the angels' message, and the two disciples hastened to the sepulchre. The apostle John, being the younger man, outstripped the elder disciple and came first to the tomb where he stood without, looking in. The older, impetuous disciple arriving rushed into the cave, and John followed him. The 8th verse of the 20th chapter of John states that John saw and believed. It is significant that the disciple whom Jesus loved was the first to accept the tremendous fact of the resurrection. John was a young man, possibly a lad still in his teens, doubtless the youngest of all the disciples, and he it was upon whom the glorious fact of the resurrection of his Lord first dawned.

It is interesting also that of the four Gospel writers only the lad John was impressed enough with the environs of the tomb to mention the garden in which it was located. The young man in the springtime of his life adds the only touch of springtime beauty and the perfume of blossoming orchards when he says, "Now in the place where He was crucified there was a garden and in the garden a new sepulchre." Only John tells us that Mary, seeing the resurrected Saviour in the garden, thought that He was the gardener. I have always wondered why she thought He was. Why should she have identified Him with the garden where He stood? Had He knelt to listen to the soundless song of resurrection pealing forth from the tiny bells of the lily-of-the-valley, which the inspired poet makes the type of Him whose loveliness is beyond compare? Had He bent to breathe a blush of new beauty upon the cheek of the rose of Sharon than which He is a thousand times more fair? Was He touching with Divine finger the delicate blossom of the almond tree to give it richer bloom and the promise of more yield? Was He blessing with the caress of His omnipotent and nail-pierced hand a withered and dead branch of an ancient olive tree to send new life coursing through that limb and clothing its nakedness with an Easter dress of dark green leaves? Had He who had not yet ascended to His Father stooped to inhale the perfume of a flower or to linger in the shade of the hedges? I wonder why she thought He was a gardener! But whatever the reason, she was right. He *is* a Gardener.

He is the Rock of Ages, the Light of the World, the Bread of Life! He is the Great High Priest, the Prince of Peace! He is God Incarnate, the One in whom dwelleth all the fulness of the Godhead bodily. He is All in All. But Mary was right; He is a Gardener, and Mary looking on the beauty of that garden through the shining of her tears that day beheld Him who is the Gardener of Eternity.

His was the hand that sowed in the azure fields of space the seeds of fire which blazed forth into astral beauty. All the planets in their courses are the flaming blossoms of His planting. He, the altogether Lovely One, the Fairest of Ten Thousand, is the Author of all beauty and the landscape Artist of creation. Every tree plucked by the fingers of the wind is a singing harp in the orchestra of His conducting. Every little flower unseen by human eye in the tangled depth of the primeval forest pays its redolent tribute of praise to the Artist who painted its colors and gave it life. Above the snow line on the mountain-top the infant blossom that pushes aside its fleecy white blanket of winter and lifts its tiny head for the breath of springtime, sings of Him, the great Gardener of the Universe.

The Book of Genesis tells us that, having made a world and all its planetary companions, having set the sun to rule over the day and the moon the night, and being now ready to make man, the Lord God planted a garden "eastward in Eden." What a lovely place it must have been, this habitation fashioned for the creature of His hand, and the man whose form He shaped from the dust of the ground from which burst all the bloom of the garden! What a beautiful place, Eden! The rocks of crystal; rubies and emeralds and topaz and zircons in ordered array bordering the garden paths and embroidering the hems of the flower beds! The rivers, clear as crystal; the breezes, cool and sweet! A perfect garden with no blight on any flower, no thorn on any rose, no mold on any leaf—a garden created for the dwelling-place of the first man in the dawn of human life. There God placed Adam, and there lulled by the aroma-laden breezes and overcome with the sweetness of its flowers, God made a deep sleep fall upon him; and awakening to the songs of the rich-plumaged tenants of its tree tops, Adam found beside him Eve for a helpmeet and companion.

No one ever had more beautiful surroundings. No one ever had an easier task than the keeping and the dressing of a garden where no leaves fell, where no flower died, and where no weeds grew.

But Adam sinned! That day were decay and destruction begotten. That day a change came over the garden. As that day drew to its close, Adam and Eve started homeward to the bower which was their bedroom and Adam was amazed to find upon the snow-white breast of the lily growing beside the path a stain of yellow, and Eve plucking a rose to twine in her hair cried out in pain and surprise and looking down beheld a sharp thorn on a stem where no thorn had ever been before. A seared leaf fluttering downward brushed Adam's cheek. On the crystal gravel of the garden walk like a great spot of blood lay the body of a red cardinal that had greeted the morning with his song. Death had come to the garden. Through the tall hedges a frightened deer fled from the leopard with which he had been grazing side by side. The springtime of that garden passed without summer into fall, and death became our heritage who are children of Adam;

and our first parents lost their garden, driven out. God "planted a garden eastward in Eden," but through man's sin the garden became a jungle and the whole earth a wilderness.

But in Judea there was another garden, a garden with an open tomb, a promise of the garden which this world shall become through the divine power of the One whose redemptive love made that garden grave for a short space the couch of the Son of God. We are told that some day all the earth will be glad and "the desert shall rejoice, and blossom as the rose." Because of Christ's victory over death the springtime of Eden shall return to earth, the perfection of the eastern garden on the threshold of Time shall come again with His return to reign upon this planet. The first Adam by his sin lost his garden. The Second Adam by His power and perfection restores a garden to the world. "The wilderness and the solitary place shall be glad." The rose, free from the thorny mark of man's fall, will lift its dainty face to greet the day, and the lilies unstained by any blemish will pour out their fragrance as an offering to the One who occupies the throne of David, the One who rose from a tomb in a garden on an Easter day. All the ruins of bomb-blasted cities, all the shell craters which pock the earth, all the scars of a thousand battlefields will be covered over by a verdant drapery embroidered with flowers in gay designs. All the rocky wastes and sandy places will sing their anthems of gladness as the breezes blow through their hedges and stir their green grasses into billows like the sea. Because a risen Saviour stepped from a tomb in a garden, all the earth shall become a garden in the glory of His risen presence when He returns to rule the creation which He made. He, the Second Adam, by the power of His own omnipotence, He, the resurrected Adam, by the power of His divine life, shall restore to all His creation the springtime life and the glory and the beauties and the odors of Eden!

But the end is not yet. For, beyond the millennial beauties of His reign, there is a new heaven and a new earth and a heavenly city—the new Jerusalem—come down from God out of heaven! There in the midst of the golden streets surrounded by jasper walls, the angelic hosts shall hear the redeemed sing the praise of the Lamb! There beside the river of the Water of Life of which the redeemed freely drink; there transplanted from Eden is the Tree of Life on each side of the stream and in the midst of the golden streets! There in the new Jerusalem is the garden whose springtime never ends, there in the midst of the city is the garden—the trees heavily laden with the fruitage of autumn, rich and plentiful—with the springtime on its leaves, which are for the healing of the nations.

But the end is not yet. For here and now in every life where the Lord Jesus Christ rules in the power of His resurrection is a garden. All the barren places of human desolation, all the desert griefs in the human heart, without a spring of water welling up, all the morasses of mortality, all the evil thickets in the mind and heart of man—all these become a bursting garden of well-ordered bloom when He dwells and reigns within. He makes the desert to rejoice and blossom as a rose, even the desert of the human heart. The autumn of the human life, the icy winters of mortal desolation within, are ended in the springtime of His resurrection power. The life, barren and useless and cursed with sin, becomes verdant and fruitful and fragrant when He is the Gardener of that life.

The Bible speaks of the fruit of the Spirit. That fruit is planted by the Holy Spirit in the garden of the heart, where the risen Saviour walks.

Love blossoms there. Love like that which animates the heart of the wild thing for its young. Love which makes the tiny bird fight to protect the fledgling in the nest. Love not centered in self, but lost in Him and those for whom He died. And it is just to the extent that you find love abounding in your life that you know Him in the fulness and the power of His resurrection.

Joy! Joy like spring ablaze with bloom, alive with perfume, filled with the song of the oriole and caressed with the breath of the south wind. Such joy blossoms in the heart which has become a garden through Him and the power of His resurrection.

Peace! Peace like a summer night vibrant with the music of the nightingale. Peace like a quiet stream between banks of lilacs and green mosses. The peace of a lovely garden on a lovely night, a garden undisturbed by the footfall of a stranger or awakened by any trespasser from beyond its bowers. That is the life, lived amid the turmoil and strife of the world, but made peaceful by His indwelling.

Longsuffering! Longsuffering like the straight, tall cedar, always green, whether it stands upon the verdant carpet under the heat of a burning sun, or whether the carpet about its feet is of snow and the blasts which burst upon it come down from the mountain tops of winter as the ice bears down its branches. Such longsuffering comes to the heart that knows the springtime joy of a risen Christ within.

Gentleness! Gentleness like the soft, cooing dove nesting upon the branch of the orchard tree amid the apple blossoms, those perfumed promises of the red and mellow harvest of the autumn. Such gentleness comes to the life that has been made a garden by His hand.

Goodness! Goodness like the goodness of ripe fruit to hungry men, like the sight of water in the desert to the sun-scorched traveller, worn and tired. Goodness pouring out through the whole life to bless those who need, and to take the Gospel of His love to those who sit in darkness and in the shadow of the tomb. Such is the power of His resurrection as it transforms the desert of a human heart into verdant beauty.

Faith! Faith like the bright garment of autumn wherewith the garden decks itself in defiance of conquering winter and the confidence of the resurrection which awaits it with the returning spring. Such is the fruit of the seed of faith planted by Him in a desolate heart.

Meekness! Meekness like the tiny violets at the feet of the giant oak; like the wee, wizened, sad faces of pansies at the roots of the giant redwood tree. Meekness low and humble, but meekness whose sweetness blesses the whole garden. That is the heritage of life wherein a resurrection garden has been planted.

Temperance! Temperance like the soft, gentle wind dimpling the dust of country lanes, refreshing the garden without breaking the tenderest stalk or bruising the most fragile blossom. That is the temperance of the life that knows Him in the power of His resurrection.

But every garden has its tomb, even the garden which He plants within the human heart, but the darkness of that tomb is made bright by the assurance that because He lives we shall live also. The glorious birth of spring depends upon the death of autumn, and the seed must be buried beneath the loam before it can burst through the dark soil in living beauty. The Gardener who plants and loves the garden is the One who sends the seasons and who plans the changes of the year. He it is who, standing in the early dawning amid the freshness of a dew-kissed garden before an open tomb, says to us who love Him, "Because I live, ye shall live also."

> Christ is risen from the dead.
> Bare the cold and stony bed,
> Cast aside the grave clothes lie,
> Bright and blue the morning sky.
> Tenantless the cruel tomb,
> Pure and white the lilies bloom.
> Risen is the One who died.
> Risen is the Crucified!
>
> Christ is risen from the dead.
> Death a captive He hath led;
> He hath broken Hell's strong chain,

Hath removed sin's crimson stain.
By His death the forfeit paid,
Fullest recompense hath made.
Fulfilled is the promised Word,
Glory to the Risen Lord!

Christ is risen from the dead.
Radiant glories crown His head;
Lord of life on earth to reign
In glory He shall come again.
His the scepter and the crown,
Angels at His feet bow down.
Hark, the heavenly anthem rings—
Christ is risen, King of kings!

HANDS AND FEET

Behold My hands and My feet, that it is I
Myself: handle Me, and see; for a ghost
hath not flesh and bones, as ye see Me
have. And when He had thus spoken *He
showed them His hands and His feet.*

—Luke 24: 39, 40.

HANDS AND FEET

GATHERED in the upper room, the dazed disciples could not comprehend the fact of the resurrection. As they listened now to the words of the men who on the road to Emmaus had walked with the risen Saviour and recognized Him in the breaking of bread at supper time, they still were unable to grasp the truth that the Lord was alive. As the voices of the witnesses of the Emmaus road died into silence, the Lord Himself appeared suddenly in their midst. What a thrill His appearing at the very climax of their narrative must have brought to these men with whom He had walked in the way! How eagerly they must have welcomed this evidence manifest in His very person of the truth that He was risen as they had been saying to the disciples.

But, not thus did the disciples look upon the familiar form. Shrinking back from His presence, they cried, "It is a ghost." To prove the reality of His resurrection presence the Lord said to them, "Behold My hands and My feet, that it is I Myself: handle Me, and see; for a ghost hath not flesh and bones, as ye see Me have. And when He had thus spoken, He showed them His hands and His feet."

We are prone to think of Thomas as the disciple of doubt, the follower of failing faith, but he was as quick to accept the resurrection and recognize the risen Lord as were the other disciples. This time he was not present, and when the others, convinced by the sight of hands and feet and side—convinced some of them possibly by touching the risen Saviour— told Thomas of having stood in the presence of the Master returned from the tomb, Thomas said, "Except I shall see in His hands the print of the nails, and put my finger into the print of the nails, and thrust my hand into His side, I will not believe." Thomas asked only that he be granted the same evidence which had convinced them, and the Lord appearing a second time to the disciples, Thomas, now being present, was granted the privilege of seeing and touching the wounds.

He showed them His hands and feet. As He drew back the long sleeves of the Eastern robe they beheld His hands, and surely they recognized them. These were the hands that, raised in beckoning, had called them from their tasks and had summoned them from their places to follow Him. These hands had beckoned, and they had risen from the table of the tax-gatherer, from the bench of fishing boat.

These were the hands of the One who came to minister, the hands which had, just a few short days before, taken a basin and a towel and washed the disciples' feet as they sat together about the Passover board. These were the hands of the One who fulfilled the covenants of God, the hands that after supper took bread and cup and gave to them to eat and drink, in testimony of the body broken and the blood shed for their redemption.

These were the Physician's hands beneath whose touch fever-filled sufferers were healed and disease destroyed. These were the hands which they had seen move with miraculous touch across lips sealed into silence, to restore to them the melody of speech. These hands had paused outside the portals of hearing, shut fast from birth, to fling aside those barred doorways and send pouring in the music of the universe. These were the hands that had drawn back the curtain of blindness which shut out light and beauty from the eyes of Bartimeus, who beholding for the first time the wonders of the created universe, was blessed at that first instant with the sight of the Creator's face.

These were the hands of the Warrior, hands so tender in blessing, but so strong in the cause of right. These were the hands that overturned the table of the money-changers in the temple, and in the firm grip of that right hand was held a whip of cords to drive out the thieves and greedy ones who trafficked in God's house.

He showed them His hands.

These were the hands of the Architect, the Architect of all creation. These were the hands of Him who conceived the intricate mechanism of the universe and who designed its perfect detail. These were the hands of the Architect who was soon to go from them and prepare a place for them, a house not made with mortal hands, eternal in the heavens. These were the hands of the Architect of the New Jerusalem, foursquare in its perfection and radiant in celestial beauty.

These were the hands of the Artist, the hands of Him who with brush of fire covers the horizon with the roseate tints of dawn and with the vermilions and purples and golds of the sunset. These were the hands of the One who touches into diverse and individual beauty every leaf of autumn and who weaves them into a carpet for hillside and valley.

These were the hands of the Musician—of the One who made the Morning Stars sing together, who put the laud in the throat of the oriole and the hymn of praise in the breast of the mounting skylark, dancing against the blue curtain of the sky his winged greeting to the day. These were the hands of Him who made the valleys sing in the richness of the harvest, the One who wrote the score for the drumbeats of the tempest, the One who puts melody in the heart bowed down with sorrow, who sets harmonies aflame amid the dull ashes of grief.

"He showed them His hands and His feet."

He showed them His hands, and drawing back the long garments falling close about the ankles, He showed them His feet. Surely, the disciples must have recognized those feet! They had sat many times about them as He, the Teacher, taught. They had followed those feet on long journeys over hillside unmarked by any path, across the pebbles on the edge of Galilee, across sandy desert spaces whose dust was never kissed by gentle shower. They had followed the prints of those feet until the prints became bloody on the way to the cross.

These were unselfish feet which had never paced pathways of pleasure, feet which had gone always where there were need and suffering and sorrow, feet which sought out the place where the poor were hungry for the Gospel and the leper cried "Unclean!" and the putrefying body of Lazarus awaited their presence before the sealed tomb.

These were lonely feet! Feet which, amid the throng or apart from the multitude, traced a path of loneliness which no other could share, and in the suffering for man's redemption trod the winepress alone.

These were feet neglected of many, but loved of some. Forgot of his host and unwashed from the stain and dust of the day, these feet had been cleansed with the tears and dried with the hair of an outcast woman. These were the feet which had been made sweet with the spikenard of the broken alabaster box, and which had staggered beneath the burden of a cross.

These were holy feet! Feet which had been swift about the Father's business, the blessed feet of Him who brought good tidings. These were victorious feet. These feet had been placed upon the neck of death, had been set in triumph to bruise the head of the serpent. These feet had "led captivity captive." These feet the Lord showed His disciples.

"He showed them His hands and His feet." Familiar hands, familiar feet, but different now. So different, bruised and wounded. In the center of each palm a nail-print. In each foot the mark of the spike.

Forty days later the Lord, ascending heavenward, departed from the disciples. Looking upward the last glimpse they caught of Him was of hands outstretched in blessing and of feet climbing an invisible stair. Their last sight of the Saviour was of wounded hands and torn feet.

Now, on the right hand of the throne of God, He bears still the marks of the cross as our

Intercessor and Advocate. In His own person He shows the evidence of the penalty which He paid for us. When Satan presents himself before God to accuse the saints—and, oh! how often he has reason to accuse—the Son, our Advocate, says, "I suffered for that sin and I paid its penalty," and a riven palm lifted or a pierced foot extended plead with an eloquence which lays claim on both the mercy and justice of God.

Some day He shall appear again from heaven, and the world which has rejected and refused Him, the world which wronged and slew Him, will recognize Him by the hands and the feet. They will look on Him whom they pierced, and the wicked shall wail because of Him. The nail-pierced feet will again be red with blood, this time not His own, but the blood of His enemies, and in power the scarred hand shall hold a rod of iron as He rules in righteousness and peace.

Amid the perfection of heaven, we shall look on His hands and His feet. There, where all is without spot to detract or blemish to mar, He will bear scars throughout eternity as a Lamb that had been slain. We shall see in His blessed hands and lovely feet the marks of our redemption and the price which our place in glory cost Him to whom all glory belongs.

There have been instances where, through meditating long upon the suffering and death of Christ, men have been reputed to have received the stigmata, likenesses of the wounds which Christ bore in head and side and hands and feet. St. Francis of Assisi is said to have been thus marked. It is certainly spiritually edifying to meditate long upon the death and suffering of Christ, but the hands and feet of the Christian can bear more blessed resemblance than this to the hands and feet of our Lord. Better the resemblance of service! Our feet are so selfish, so occupied with idle goings and vain comings again; so swift in running into mischief, so slow and leaden in service. Our hands are so idle or, if busy, so busy with the weaving of empty plans and the fondling of selfish toys; so greedy in getting, so slow in giving; so eager to grasp, so reluctant to turn loose.

Behold His hands and His feet, then look at your own, and pray that yours may become like His in beauty of service and of love. May He, whose feet went the way of Calvary for us and whose hands were nailed in our stead to the cross, make our feet swift in carrying the story of His love and our hands strong to bear His cross.

The shame He suffered left its brand
In gaping wound in either hand;
Sin's penalty He deigned to meet
Has torn and scarred His blessed feet;
The condemnation by Him borne
Marred His brow with print of thorn.
Trespass and guilt for which He died
Have marked Him with a riven side.

Mine was the shame, the penalty;
The sin was mine; it was for me
He felt the nails, the thorns, the spear.
For love of me the scars appear
In hands and feet and side and brow.
Beholding them I can but bow
Myself a living sacrifice
To Him who paid so dear a price.

WHY STAND YE GAZING?

And while they looked steadfastly toward heaven as He went up, behold, two men stood by them in white apparel; which also said, Ye men of Galilee, *why stand ye gazing* up into heaven? this same Jesus, which is taken up from you into heaven, shall so come in like manner as ye have seen Him go into heaven.

—Acts 1: 10, 11.

WHY STAND YE GAZING?

THE Lord had appeared to His disciples after
His death and by "many infallible proofs,"
by incontrovertible evidence, had established
the truth of His resurrection so definitely that
even in our day, nineteen centuries later, those
who refuse to recognize Him as the Lord of
their lives must, if they examine the evidence
and are logical in their thinking, be convinced
that Christ came forth from the tomb.

Being seen of many following His resurrection, the Lord led the disciples out from Jerusalem to the Mount of Olives, and there departed from them into heaven. What a spot
from which to take His leave of them! To this
mount, made sacred to the disciples by the fellowship which they so often had enjoyed with
Him there, to the summit where the Master had
wept over Jerusalem; to the hillside in whose
garden He had spent His last hours with them
before His betrayal, and from whose slope He
had been led away for trial and crucifixion; to
this mount He brought them now, and on its
brow He left them, ascending up into heaven.
On this eminence, as they gazed after the ascended Saviour, two men in white apparel stood
beside the disciples to inquire of them, "Why
stand ye gazing up into heaven?"

The question might well be asked of many of the most devoted of the followers of Christ today. There is nothing easier than to stand gazing idly upward; and some who are well acquainted with the glorious truth of the Lord's return to earth, but who are doing nothing to hasten His return, might well ponder the question asked the disciples.

That this same Jesus will so return in like manner as His disciples saw Him go up, is a glorious truth thrilling to the heart of all who love the Lord. He left the disciples with the comfort of His promise, "I go to prepare a place for you. And if I go and prepare a place for you, I will come again, and receive you unto Myself; that where I am, there ye may be also." Through John, in the words of the Revelation, He speaks to us, "Behold, I come quickly." That we have definite commissions from our Lord to occupy us until His return, we sometimes forget.

The last recorded question which the disciples asked the Saviour before His ascension was this: "Lord, wilt Thou at this time restore again the kingdom of Israel?" The answer of the Saviour was clear and explicit. "It is not for you to know the times or the seasons, which the Father hath put in His own power"; but He added, "Ye shall receive power, after that the Holy Ghost is come upon you: and ye shall be witnesses unto Me both in Jerusalem, and in all Judæa, and Samaria, and unto the uttermost part of the earth," and with these words —and the commission to go into all the world and preach the Gospel—He left them. They were not to tarry on the mount gazing heavenward. They were to go back to Jerusalem to wait the anointing of the Holy Spirit and immediately afterwards to begin their task of witnessing.

The disciples were commissioned to *witness* to the Lord's resurrection, to testify that they had personally seen Him and talked with Him who had returned from the grave. It is our task to witness also to His resurrection life and His resurrection power in our lives. The disciples had known Him intimately for three years before His crucifixion. We who are saved know Him as the risen One. It was not our privilege to be associated with Him in His ministry, to behold the manifestations of His Deity in the miracles performed on hillside and seashore, in city streets and dusty village roads; but every one of us who is born again has met and seen and heard the risen Saviour. We have had somewhere a personal contact with Him. It is our duty now to witness to the power of His resurrection and to testify to the fact that Christ is the risen Son of God because we know Him in the power of His resurrection in our own lives. Have you met Him? Has He talked with you? Do you know Him, the risen Son of God? If so, however humble you may be, however lacking in facility of speech, however timid, however reluctant to speak out, you are commissioned to be a witness for the Lord Jesus. Any believer who is not a witness is a believer who is not living up to the commission which Christ has given Him.

In any court of law secondhand or hearsay evidence is not admitted to the record. A witness must speak of the thing that he himself has heard and seen; and unless you have met the Lord Jesus personally and have personally heard His voice, you cannot witness of Him.

A witness is not responsible for the result of his testimony. His responsibility is to speak the truth. The Lord does not ask you to produce results by your witnessing. He will take care of the results, but you must not compromise the testimony. Only eternity can disclose the full power of a faithful testimony. Sometimes a testimony which we think has gone unheeded and unnoticed brings, years later, results which surprise us.

A great New England preacher once promised to fill the pulpit of a country church on a certain Sunday. That Sunday New England was held in the grip of a blizzard. Roads were almost impassable. The preacher thought to himself, "There is no use in my going out to that church. No one will come out through such a storm. There will be nobody to preach to." But, being a conscientious man, he went. Setting out on his journey quite early, he was finally able to make his way on horseback through the snowdrifts, and arrived a few minutes before the time of worship. Stabling his horse in a shed behind the church, he entered the deserted building, built a fire, and went up into the pulpit. Precisely on the hour the service was to begin, one man entered the church and sat down at the back. The preacher wondered whether or not he should go ahead with the service in the presence of a congregation of one. Finally, he announced the hymn, and the occupant of the pew and the occupant of the pulpit sang it together. The preacher prayed, another hymn was sung, and the service proceeded just as if the church had been filled with worshipers. At the close of his message the minister pronounced the benediction, intending to speak to his "congregation" afterwards; but when he had spoken the final "Amen" and opened his eyes, the man was gone.

Twenty years later out in Ohio a stranger came up to the New England minister. "Do you remember me?" he said. "You and I spent an hour and a half together alone in a blizzard twenty years ago.   I was saved that day under your preaching of the Gospel. Now, I also am a preacher, and within this state there are a half dozen men standing in pulpits who were saved under my ministry. All this has come because you were faithful in witnessing when the testimony must have seemed to you of little value."

While the follower of Christ is not responsible for the results which his testimony produces, he is responsible to live a life that will prove the truth of his words. As followers of Christ we must live like people who have met a risen Saviour. James throws out this striking challenge, "Show me thy faith without thy works, and I will show thee my faith by my works." The evidence of any witness in court is discredited when another witness takes the stand and testifies that he knows the witness to be unreliable and dishonest and unworthy of credence. There are many Christians today whose lives and characters witness against them in their profession of a Christian experience. Unless there is in your life something of the sweetness which characterizes the Saviour, something of His humility and gentleness and longsuffering and mercy, you cannot be very well acquainted with Him. It is an old, old saying, one so trite that it should possibly be left unrepeated here, but it is none the less true, that "What you are speaks so loud, that I cannot hear what you say." You cannot know Him in the power of His resurrection life without a newness of life yourself and your works lend weight to your witness.

Our churches resound and echo with sermons about "bringing in the Kingdom." We cannot bring in the Kingdom, but we can hasten the return of the King, and when the King returns He will establish the Kingdom. His command is, "Occupy until I come." There is work to be done; the Bride of Christ must be gathered in before the Lord returns. That also is our task.

The risen Saviour, seated at the "right hand of the Majesty on high," is working the work of intercession for us. He is also preparing us a place there. We are to *work* for Him here. Some students of prophecy, who spend their time dealing with the question of the times and the seasons, who attempt to determine the exact moment of His return, would be better occupied with the work of preaching the Gospel and bringing men and women into a saving knowledge of Christ. This will hasten the day when He shall appear, for "out of every kindred, and tongue, and people, and nation" is to be gathered the Bride of Christ, who shall reign with Him upon the earth.

The Lord also commands His disciples to *watch* for His return. Watching is not the same thing as gazing. The gazing disciples stood entranced, staring upward. The watchful disciple expects the return of the Lord and is on the lookout for His appearing while he goes about the business of the Lord for whom he watches. We are told that the coming of the Lord will be as a thief in the night. It should be, therefore, as for the coming of the thief that we should watch for His appearing. Men do not watch for a thief, the hour of whose coming they cannot anticipate, by sitting up all night gun in hand. They watch for a thief by anticipating His coming in bolting the door and latching the screens on the windows. Then, they go to bed and sleep. We are not to watch for the coming of the Lord by putting on ascension robes and perching in the tree-tops. We are to watch for the Lord by doing each day's task in expectation of His coming. We watch for the Lord's return by being so faithful to our work that should He appear at any moment He would find us ready for the sound of the trump and the sight of His face. There is no better way to watch for the coming of the Lord than to finish the day's task and lie down to sleep with a clear conscience, knowing the job is done. Then, if His voice saying, "Come up hither," should awake us, we would not leave behind unfinished the task of the day before. How different this attitude from that of the technical saint who is so busy gazing up, so occupied with the signs of the times, that he is of no use to the Lord in the proclamation of the Gospel which prepares man for His appearing and hastens that day!

We must also *wait* for the coming of the Lord. We must wait for His coming to see an end of war and the beginning of a reign of peace. We must wait for His coming to bring a rule of righteousness and justice on the earth. Only the coming of the Lord Jesus will bring to pass the golden age which some men are striving so hard in the strength of the flesh to build on earth, and whose efforts mock them as they see their plans ruined and destroyed while they are still no more than dreams. We are to wait for His coming for the avenging of our wrongs, and how many of us are not willing to wait! We are to wait for His coming for the justification of the position which we have taken and of the testimony for which we stand, and how hard it is to wait! We are to be "patient," says James, "unto the coming of the Lord." Patience is a virtue to which we can attain only with much suffering and tribulation. The waiting needs reserves of spiritual resources.

Witness, work, watch, wait—all these we are commanded to do, but there is one thing yet. We are to *want* His coming, to desire it with all our hearts. John, having had revealed to him all the glories of the Revelation, all those promises of the Lord's return, with heartfelt, personal longing cries out, "Even so, come Lord Jesus." That He will come is sure. That the time is short seems likely. By your desire for the Day of the Lord you can gauge the purity of your love for Him. By the eagerness of your heart to see His face you can measure the reality of your surrender. Do you long for His presence? If there is anything you want more than you want His appearing, you do not wholly love Him.

A woman, greatly excited, came up to a preacher at the close of a message on the Second Coming of the Lord, exclaiming, "You said He might come this year. He cannot come this year. There are things I want to do; and if He comes this year, that will interfere with my plans." If you have any dream that is more precious than the sight of His face, you are not a yielded, consecrated Christian. The coming of the Lord is referred to as a "glorious hope" and "every man that hath this hope in him purifieth himself, even as He is pure." The deep desire for the appearing of the Lord comes only from a heart that is pure and ready for the gaze of His searching eye. The desire for the return of the Lord stimulates the Christian to service and to the ministry of the Gospel and to a faithfulness of testimony for the hastening of His coming. To want Him to appear means to watch, to greet each day with the thought, "perhaps He will come today," to lie down to sleep each night with the eager anticipation of awakening to meet Him in the starry heavens.

This same Jesus shall so come in like manner as you have seen Him go up—visibly, personally, physically. He will come! Be faithful to the tasks which He has given to His disciples to perform that at His coming you may not be ashamed. "Why stand ye gazing up?"

TO WHOM SHALL WE GO?

Then said Jesus unto the twelve, Will ye also go away? Then Simon Peter answered Him, Lord, *to whom shall we go?* Thou hast the words of eternal life.

—John 6: 67, 68.

TO WHOM SHALL WE GO?

THE faithless fell from the ranks. From the time they discovered that all was not to be a pathway strewn with roses over which they should follow the Saviour to power and prominence, many deserted Him. "From that time many of His disciples went back, and walked no more with Him. Then said Jesus unto the twelve, Will ye also go away? Then Simon Peter answered Him, Lord, to whom shall we go? Thou hast the words of eternal life."

And to whom shall *we* go if not to Christ? He hath still the words of eternal life. The urge to live is innate in the human heart. Men cling to life. The instinct of self-preservation asserts itself in the actions of the poorest, most bestial savage and in the unconscious intellectual processes of the most civilized. Love of life and the determination to secure as much as possible of satisfaction and pleasure from each of its fleeting moments are universal. The desire for death is not the normal attitude on the part of any individual. Man in a normal state of mind flees the dark-robed figure and leering, fleshless face of Death. Stunned by grief, crazed by pain, discouraged by disappointment and hardship, some seek his skeleton arms, not knowing that not death but more life—life in Christ—is the answer to their anguish and the relief from their pain.

> So weary souls that crave for death,
>   As sweet and dreamless sleep,
> As night when men may cease to war
>   And women cease to weep
> Are longing still for life—more life,
>   Their souls not yet sufficed,
> Cry out for God's eternal streams;
>   They crave not death—but Christ.*

Christ completely satisfies the hunger and meets the desire for fulness of life. "I am come that they might have life, and that they might have it more abundantly," says He. Oh, that man would learn that full joy and satisfaction abound only in Him! If this life were all, if there were nothing beyond our brief day but darkness, sleep undisturbed by any dream, unhaunted by any feverish apparition, with no awakening at gray dawn in the birth of another day beyond the night of the tomb—if this life were all—Christ only is the Fountain from which man may drink the draught of abundance.

But, this life is not all. Beyond the dark vale of mortality, beyond the valley of the shadow, lies eternity where the high white

---

* G. A. Studdert Kennedy.

hills of eternal life with Christ rise above the dark morasses and fathomless gorges of eternal death without Him. He only hath the words of eternal life. "There is none other name under heaven given among men, whereby we must be saved," than the matchless name of Christ. "I am the Way, the Truth, and the Life: no man cometh unto the Father, but by Me," said the Saviour; and the apostle John writing under the inspiration of the Holy Spirit said, "For God so loved the world, that He gave His only begotten Son, that whosoever believeth in Him should not perish, but have everlasting life."

Where shall we go for *salvation*, if not to Him? To whom shall we look for forgiveness of sin and life eternal if not to Jesus Christ, the Son of God? We may study the philosophies of ancient sages; we may drink at the fountain of the wisdom of the seers—and find the waters often not lucent pure, but muddy and defiled; we may examine the achievements of scientists and pause in amazement before the marvels which rise like monuments to their faithfulness in research or their good fortune in discovery; but only Jesus hath the words of eternal life. Others may point to paths of ethical conduct. Others may offer philosophical opiates for the disease of sin, but only God's Son can say, "Because I live, ye shall live also."

To whom shall we go with the needs of our life? Who else but the Giver of life is able to satisfactorily meet its problems?

To whom shall we go for *victory* in the hour of temptation? Who else but the omnipotent God can subdue the overwhelming tides of desire which rush in to drown the soul? Who but Christ Jesus can defeat the power of Satan when he comes strong in evil to make war upon the life? Who else but God's Son can give to us the power to stand under the volcanic blasts from hell which bear down upon us with titanic fury? To whom else shall we go for victory in the hour when flesh is weak and temptation strong? Where else shall we go but to Him who "Himself hath suffered being tempted" and hath proved that "He is able to succor them that are tempted"? He only is able to provide the way of escape!

To whom shall we go for *strength* in the time of weakness than to Him whose strength is made perfect in our weakness? To whom can the toiler turn for rest but to Christ? A carpenter in the shop of Nazareth, given to hard travel and long journeys, buffeted by the elements, exhausted with the work of ministry and of miracle, He knew the weariness that seizes the muscles until every part of the body seems ablaze with pain. Wrestling in the anguish of the Garden, covered with drops of blood like sweat, He knew the weariness of the struggle of the soul. He is no idle philosopher discoursing on the beauty of labor and the strength derived from toil. He is God's Son saying, "Come unto Me, all ye that labour and are heavy laden, and I will give you rest. Take My yoke upon you and learn of Me; for I am meek and lowly in heart: and ye shall find rest unto your souls. For My yoke is easy, and My burden is light." And to His own, like an ever-swelling chord of music down the centuries, come the divine words spoken by this One centuries before His advent to His servant Moses, "My presence shall go with thee, and I will give thee rest."

To whom shall we go for *wisdom* but to Him "who of God is made unto us wisdom"? Human wisdom is weak; human philosophies are but frail and futile lances of straw that break against the dragon problems that confront us. In his attempt by his own wisdom to solve the problems of his life, man is mocked by failure. No institution born of human wisdom approaches perfection. No brain child is immortal. For centuries man has sought the solution of the problems of human wretchedness and woe, the problems of war and of disease, the problems of international differences, the problems of human greed; sought, and thought he had within his grasp; sought, and found what seemed for a moment to work; sought, and failed to discover a full and lasting answer. To whom shall we go but to Him "in whom are hid all the treasures of wisdom and knowledge"? To whom shall we go but to the Source of all wisdom, to the One who presented in one crystal clear sentence the answer for which men, refusing to heed Him, have wasted centuries searching—"Seek ye first the kingdom of God, and His righteousness; and all these things shall be added unto you."

In their darkness men have groped for light; from the friction of conflicting opinions struck themselves sparks which flashed and died. Philosophers have lighted candles which flickered for a moment and were blown out by the breath from the wings of the bats of human depravity. Where in our darkness shall we find light but in Him who said, "I am the Light of the world," where but in Him who is the "true Light, which lighteth every man that cometh into the world"? From whence shall the dawn come to dispel the darkness of the starless night of human ignorance and sin if not from the "Sun of Righteousness," risen with "healing in His wings"?

To whom shall we go for *confidence*? All about is uncertainty and change. We sojourn in a crumbling house, a ruined city. Popularity dies, riches fly, fame fades, friends desert. In what can we fix our hope? In whom confide but Him? The dreams of our youth mock us in our age. The cup whose first draft was sweet grows bitter in the dregs. He who seemed to our blind eyes the Moses to lead us from our wilderness into a land of plenty, proved traitor to our trust. Those who seemed angels of Light proved often minions of Darkness. Men have fixed their confidence elsewhere and have been mocked or betrayed, left deserted and forlorn. To whom shall we go in confidence, save to Him who never uttered word untrue and who said, "I will never leave thee, nor forsake thee. . . . Lo, I am with you alway, even unto the end of the world"? Amid shifting scenes and changing situations, where find a refuge unchanging, sure, but at His side who is "the same yesterday, today, and forever"?

> Change and decay in all around I see;
> O Thou who changest not, abide with me!*

When our hearts are broken with sorrow and torn with grief, to whom shall we go for *comfort*? The room of sorrow is a room wherein each mortal dwells alone. No two griefs are identical. No two men lose in a loved one exactly the same. In a sense one who has lost a mother can somewhat understand the sorrow

---

* H. F. Lyte.

of another whose mother has been taken away, but the griefs are not identical. The capacity for suffering in the two hearts is not the same. The devotion of the two hearts to the ones of whom they have been bereaved varies in intensity. Reaching out to clasp the hand of the suffering one in the hour of his anguish, the arm of human sympathy is short. Only He can fully share our sorrow who knows fully our heart. Only the Lord Jesus Christ can see the secret places of the soul. To whom shall we go for comfort but to Him who enters into the fellowship of all human suffering, to Him who is "the Man of sorrows and acquainted with grief"? Was ever anguish like His anguish, was ever suffering so great as His who wept in compassion over Jerusalem and poured out the treasure of His tears at the tomb of Lazarus? To whom shall we go for comfort but to Him who is able to wipe away our tears? Who can provide surcease from sorrow save Him who bids us weep no more, and who in the power of His resurrection, assures the restoration of the loved one to our side? To whom shall we go for comfort but to Him?

Where may *peace* be found? Not in the council chambers where statesmen sit jealous of the rights of their own nations, cutting themselves niches in the wall of history. Not in the signature of sovereigns who with the ink scarcely dry on the peace paper prepare war and plot new conquests. Where shall we go for peace amid the differences of opinions, the diversities of ideas, the clash of ambitions and the conflicts of thought? Where may we find peace in a war-torn world? We may "seek peace and pursue it," but never find nor overtake. To whom shall we go for peace if not to the Prince of Peace? The warrior's ear, deafened by the broil of battle, has not caught His Word. Kings and princes, their hearing occupied with the clamor of their own ambitions, greedy, ambitious men, their auditory senses hammered by the voices of bitterness and hatred, have down the centuries been deaf to His voice speaking peace. "Peace I leave with you, My peace I give unto you: not as the world giveth, give I unto you. Let not your heart be troubled, neither let it be afraid." Hear the words from His lips! Only He gives peace amid the conflict, only He will bring peace out of the endless conflict of the ages. Only He, the Prince of Peace, is the Author of peace. He has had no seat at our peace tables, He has had no part in our peace programs. We have sought peace and not found her because she dwells with Him.

To whom shall we go for *joy*? He is the Giver of song. In His presence sorrow and sighing flee away and joy and gladness soar on mounting wing. All other melodies jangle "out of tune and harsh" save those set singing by His hand. Where shall we go for joy? Not to the pleasures of the flesh, which last but for a moment, clothing in bright garments dissolution and decay. Not to riches, which quickly flee away and even while they linger buy not joy nor happiness. Not to learning, which at first is an intoxication and becomes "a weariness of the flesh." Not to fame, whose demands, as heavy as the granite on which she carves our names, weigh down the soul. Not to glory, whose trailing mantle obliterates the names she stoops to write upon the sands. To whom shall we go for joy but to Him in whose presence there is fulness of joy and at whose right hand are pleasures forevermore?

To whom shall we go but to Christ, who answers every need, who is the inexhaustible supply? Who else can grant and what other welcomes? Where shall we turn but toward the sound of His voice and the sight of His face, where hasten but toward His outstretched hands and welcoming smile, where bring our need but to His fulness, where speed but to the embrace of His love? To whom shall we go but to Him who, ascended in the beauty of His resurrection to the glory on high, sends back to all the sons of earth the invitation, "Whosoever will, let Him come!"

NO MORE SEA

And I saw a new heaven and a new earth:
for the first heaven and the first earth were
passed away; and *there was no more sea.*

—Revelation 21: 1.

NO MORE SEA

JOHN, the disciple whom Jesus loved, was now an old man past seventy. The others of the apostolic company were all dead, and John only remained. Weary with years and ripe in service, he had been exiled to the island of Patmos. Far from the place of his youth and the scenes of his childhood, he knew none of the comforts to which we are accustomed to consider old age entitled. No friendly fireside welcomed his withered limbs. No strong sons in the maturity of their manhood cared for his needs. No grandchild sat on his knee or begged for bedtime stories.

John, the disciple whom Jesus loved when as a lad he had leaned upon the breast of the Saviour at supper and stood beside his mother at the foot of the cross, was still John the beloved. The hardships of these latter years were among the "all things" that "work together for good to them that love God, to them who are the called according to His purpose." John, who had not been put upon the shelf useless and bound by the strands of his years to idleness, beheld flashing across the cliff-tops of the isle of exile the grandeur of the Revelation. Because John was "in the spirit on the Lord's day" on the isle called Patmos, the servant of

God, called of the Lord, we have through him the Apocalyptic Book. John it was whom God chose to set down the account of things to come, and for this vision God had permitted him to come to loneliness and exile in his old age.

John saw the end-times, the earth in upheaval, pestilence, famine, and war. He glimpsed the rapture of the Church, the time of the tribulation, the mounting powers of evil, the revelation of the Man of Sin, the return of the Lord in glory to put all things under His feet. Before his wondering gaze stretched the thousand years of millennial magnificence under the reign of God's Son, the Prince of Peace. Then, in his vision, Satan being loosed for a little season and rebellion and iniquity breaking forth again, John beheld the final victory of the Lord's Christ and the judgment of the great White Throne.

Finally, John beheld the very earth itself, the theatre of the iniquitous deeds of man through all the years of his history, destroyed in the consuming fire of divine wrath. The very atmosphere which had resounded to the cursings and echoed to the blasphemies of sinful man shared in the cleansing and purifying flame. Planets, like loosened gems, fell from their sockets. The moon, red as blood, was wiped from the sky, the sun destroyed. And then, the first heaven and the first earth hav-

ing passed away, John beheld a new heaven and
rief is his description of it.
tion of towering mountains or
ns. He says not a word about
ndscape or the verdure where-
There is no reference to the
ens or to the intricate pattern
s and of open meadows. John
, that "there was no more sea."
exile was surrounded by the sea.
the screaming of the seagulls be-
had lifted the veil of mists from
atmos. Standing on the topmost
y direction he beheld the sea in all
moods and varied colors. On still,
hts the maiden moon smiled at her
the sea's great mirror of cerulean
ter rode down from the North in a
spray across its angry billows. He
ace of ocean in its laughing mood
little wavelets, like frisky kittens,
with strands of seaweed about the
the beach. On stormy nights John,
ning's flashes, glimpsed the bosom of
heaving in anger beneath the insults
vind and the lashing of the tempest. He
ed the pouting tides pull their lacy gowns
oam about them, turn their backs and sulk
away from the beach. He watched the enamored billows fling themselves upon the

rocky breast of those chaste shores and, being repulsed, die of love unrequited, to be trampled under foot of their fellow waves as they in their turn rushed up to kiss the sands. Always he lived surrounded with the sight and sound and smell of the sea. Neptune was his jailer. He was bound in with water bands, enclosed by the ocean as by the granite of a prison cell. "As a moat defensive to a house" the imprisoning sea fenced in the lonely, ancient, Beloved Disciple. No wonder then that beholding the new heaven and the new earth, he noted the absence of ocean's face. No wonder then that he was quick to record the fact that in the new earth "there was no more sea!" How deep he must have dipped pen into ink, how heavily have pressed it into the parchment as he wrote: "There was no more sea"!

The sea speaks of mystery and fear. To the mariner of ancient times, who braved the terrors of the deep and voyaged beyond the sight of familiar shores, all about were unknown terrors. In strange waters hungry reefs lay in wait with jagged teeth to gnaw at his vessel's keel. The mists "spumed of the wild sea's snorting" hid treacherous rocks and dangerous whirlpool. His imagination peopled the dark waters with awful monsters and strange creatures.

In these our days the sea is still mysterious

and fearsome. When great nations are locked in war, steel submarines, great leviathans of the deep, spew forth destruction upon unwary vessel and helpless crew; and floating mines, like creatures spawned in Hell and let loose upon the bosom of the deep, wait to caress with touch of death the hull of man-of-war or dirty merchant tramp.

Ocean's floor is rich with the treasures of forgotten empires and of unremembered kings. Pearls and rubies, covered by the currents with the sands, intermingle with coral-crusted bones of drowned seamen far down where sun's rays never penetrate. Proud ships lie twisted, battered hulks on rocky ledge and in unfathomed fissures of ocean's bed. They sailed beyond the sight of watchers on the shore and never reached the port toward which they voyaged. Unheard of more, they rest additional mysteries locked in ocean's hold.

Our lives are full of fears and perplexity. There are fears of things which never come to pass, dread of dangers which we never meet. The mystery of God's dealings with His own, the whys and wherefores of the Divine plan, perplex the saint even while he trusts the Father's love. The future which he cannot see frightens the saint of little faith.

But, in the new earth prepared for the site of God's city come down from heaven, there is no sea to devour men and treasure, no hidden rocks and lurking, unseen dangers. No clouds rise where there is no ocean to give them birth, and in His presence we shall stand where all hidden things have been revealed and all mystery vanished, where there is no more sea. The things which we have been unable to understand here, a loving Father will make plain to us there.

It was peeping through the brambles, that little wild white rose,
Where the hawthorn hedge was planted, my garden to enclose.
All beyond was fern and heather on the breezy, open moor,
All within was sun and shelter, and the wealth of beauty's store.
But I did not heed the fragrance of flow'ret or of tree;
For my eyes were on that rosebud, and it grew too high for me.
In vain I strove to reach it through the tangled mass of green,
It only smiled and nodded behind its thorny screen.
Yet through that summer morning I lingered near the spot:
Oh, why do things seem sweeter if we possess them not?
My garden buds were blooming, but all that I could see
Was that little mocking wild rose hanging just too high for me.

So in life's wider garden there are buds of promise, too,
Beyond our reach to gather, but not beyond our view;
And like the little charmer that tempted me astray,
They steal out half the brightness of many a summer's
    day.
Oh, hearts that fail with longing for some forbidden
    tree,
Look up and learn a lesson from my wild white rose
    and me.

'Tis wiser far to number the blessings at my feet
Than ever to be sighing for just one bud more sweet.
My sunbeams and my shadows fall from a pierced hand,
I can surely trust His wisdom since His heart I under-
    stand;
And maybe in the morning, when His blessed face I
    see,
He will tell me why my white rose grew just too high
    for me.*

The sea speaks also of time and of change. The tides are the great clepsydra, the water clock, of our earth, and by their rise and fall they mark the passing of the days and the onward rush of years. The protean seascapes, ever varying, are like the changes which the years bring to men's lives. How the years mark us as they come and go! They leave their footprints in little wrinkles in the corner of the eye. Maliciously they pinch creases in our cheeks. They mark us with the touch of death on the back of our hands and in the sagging

---

* Ellen H. Willis.

lines of throat and neck. Some of us on the voyage of life gather pounds like barnacles; others, like craft drawn up on the beach in the sun, dry up and gape open at the seams. But whether we grow burdened with the weight of flesh or withered and wasted away, the years set their mark upon us.

One of the sad things in life is this, that when we have grown rich in experience we grow weak in strength. By the time we have accumulated the knowledge and training which would make us fully useful, we have grown too old to serve. When we have become completely conscious of the opportunities and needs about us, and when our talents have reached their maturity of development, nighttime comes upon us, and we lie down to sleep the sleep of death.

There in the new earth no tides will mark with wet fingers the glittering sands before the Holy City to record the passing of the hours, for John beheld a great angel stand at the last upon this our present earth with one foot on the sea and one foot on the land and swear that time shall be no more. In the new earth there is no time and no ever-changing, temperamental sea to speak symbolically of the changes which time brings into the lives of men.

Who of us but longs to recall days buried under the rubble of the years! Who does not long to walk again amid vanished scenes the ways of childhood! Who of us, if he could re-live the past, would not live it differently!

> Break, break, break!
>   At the foot of thy crags, O sea!
> But the tender grace of a day that is dead
>   Will never come back to me.*

All is fleeting here, shifting, changing; but all there is fixed, unchanging, eternal. In the strength of eternal youth, in the richness of transfigured maturity, there we shall run and not grow weary, and if, in His divine wisdom, the Lord sets us to labor for Him there, we shall not faint under any burden nor grow too old for the task.

The sea in the Bible is sometimes the type of sin. The prophet Isaiah tells us "the wicked are like the troubled sea, when it cannot rest, whose waters cast up mire and dirt." Here we are always in the presence of sin. It is as universal as the sea. Saved by the blood of the Lord Jesus Christ and freed from the penalty of sin, we still dwell with its presence all about us. Trusting for victory in His grace, we may live above the power of sin and find freedom from its dominion over our lives. We, none-the-less remain in its presence. It manifests itself in a thousand ways, in broken lives and blighted homes, in wars and tumults, in famines and hatreds. On every hand sin raises

---

* Alfred Lord Tennyson.

its ugly head. The disease of sin has pock-marked the face of the earth and cursed this creation, but there sin shall never enter nor anything that makes unclean. And the sea, by its absence, reminds us that sin, too, is absent. The golden sands of the new earth will never be marked by mire and dirt cast up by the sea, and no life there shall be marred or blighted by sin.

> Our sins, alas, how strong they be!
>   And like a violent sea
> They break our duty, Lord, to Thee,
>   And hurry us away.
>
> The waves of trouble, how they rise!
>   How loud the tempests roar!
> But storm and wrack shall never beat
>   Upon that heavenly shore.
>
> There to fulfil His sweet commands
>   Our speedy feet shall move;
> No sin shall clog our winged zeal,
>   Or cool our burning love.
>
> There shall we sit, and sing, and tell
>   The wonders of His grace,
> Till heavenly raptures fire our hearts,
>   And smile in every face.
>
> For ever His dear sacred name
>   Shall dwell upon our tongue,
> And Jesus and Salvation be
>   The close of every song.*

---

* Isaac Watts (alt.).

In the Word of God the sea is also the symbol of judgment. The second verse of the first chapter of Genesis tells us that "darkness was upon the face of the deep." Creation was under God's judgment. Originally created in a perfect state, the curse of deep waters had been placed upon it because of sin. It may have been the sin of Lucifer and his hosts who, being cast out of heaven, came upon this earth, which brought down God's wrath; but whatever the reason, the waters that covered the earth beneath the darkness were God's judgment upon the planet. Again, in the time of Noah the waters were poured out and all the race save only Noah and his family were destroyed in the flood. We have God's promise that never again shall all flesh be consumed by the waters, but the sea reminds us that God judges sin. The final judgment upon this earth will be a judgment of fire, and then, all sin having been judged, there will be no need of judgment in the new earth, nor any sea to remind us of God's condemnation of unrighteousness.

The sea separates and divides continent from continent, and island from mainland; and the sea typifies the division of the human race into multitudes and nations and tongues and peoples. Like the cross-currents of the sea, national ideologies conflict, national ambitions clash wave upon wave. The sea of the earth is stormy and tumultuous as nation rises against nation. Hatred, misunderstanding and war stir and shake the earth. But, in that new earth there will be neither nationalities nor national boundaries. No longer French and Italian and German and Japanese and American; no longer black and white and yellow and red speaking varied tongues and different dialects; we shall be all one, members of the same family—of the household of God. No longer will men of different nations be enemies, but they shall dwell together as brethren in the mansions prepared on that sea-less shore. No longer shall color of skin and cast of countenance mark differences of race and blood, but all shall be like Him, having seen Him as He is. No babble of tongues shall shatter with discord the harmony of heaven, but all shall blend together in the anthems of glory, in the song of Moses and the Lamb.

Here, where the seas divide and separate, mothers kiss their sons good-by and see them sail away to foreign shores. Separated by thousands of miles of water, they never meet again. There, there is no separation, but eternal fellowship. Differences divide here. Men and women dwelling under the same roof together are sometimes worlds apart in sympathy and understanding, but there we shall know even as we are known, and in the light of His presence we shall understand each other and be no more divided by strife, and differences, and misunderstandings.

The cold waters of the sea remind us of the cold tide of death. And there, where is no sea, is no death. The last enemy having been conquered, the hillsides of the new earth will never be marked with granite slab or marble monument or funereal cypress. No funeral procession will pass down the golden streets. The gates of pearl will never stand open for a cortège of death. Never more shall we, having lost a loved one, see something which we know would interest him and in our eagerness think, "Oh, I must tell him of that," and then with sinking heart remember that he has passed beyond the sound of our voice and the touch of our hand. There, none shall see a loved one slip away in eventide upon the sea of death. None shall feel the fog in his throat nor pass through the waters of sorrow. There is no death, nor sorrow, nor crying, for the former things are passed away and all is new in the new earth under the new heaven where there is no more sea.

There is no ocean pounding upon the barriers of the shores in the new earth; but there is a vessel before the throne of God, typified by the brazen laver in the tabernacle of the wilderness and in the temple of Jerusalem. This vessel, called in the Revelation "a sea of glass like unto crystal," speaks of the washing of the Word by the Holy Spirit and the blood of Christ. There, in the midst of the new Jerusalem it stands, reminding us of the love that bought us and brought us citizens to the heavenly city and inhabitants to the new earth. Through eternity we shall behold it and praise Him that we of Zion's city are citizens through matchless grace and redemptive blood.

And proceeding out of the throne of God and the Lamb there is a river clear as crystal, the river of the water of life, of which the redeemed drink freely. But here in our earth now, any who will may partake of that immortal stream. The Spirit and the Bride say, "Come. And let him that heareth say, Come. And let him that is athirst come. And whosoever will, let him take the Water of Life freely." The Lord Jesus says, "Whosoever drinketh of the water that I shall give him shall never thirst; but the water that I shall give him shall be in him a well of water springing up into everlasting life."

> I heard the voice of Jesus say,
>   "Behold, I freely give
> The living water; thirsty one,
>   Stoop down, and drink, and live!"
> I came to Jesus, and I drank
>   Of that life-giving stream;
> My thirst was quenched, my soul **revived,**
>   And now I live in Him.*

* Horatius Bonar